Grand Diplôme® Cooking Course

Volume 12

Grand Diplôme® Cooking Course

A Danbury Press Book

The Danbury Press

a division of Grolier Enterprises, Inc.

Robert B. Clarke   Publisher

This book has been adapted from the Grand Diplôme Cooking Course, originally published by Purnell Cookery, U.S.A.

Purnell Grand Diplôme Editorial Board

Rosemary Hume and Muriel Downes
Principals, London Cordon Bleu Cookery
School, England

Anne Willan	Editor
Eleanor Noderer	Associate Editor
Sheryl Julian	Assistant Editor
John Paton	Managing Editor
José Northey	Co-ordinating Editor
Peter Leather	Art Editor
Charles F. Turgeon	Wine Consultant
Joy Langridge	Consultant Editor

Library of Congress Catalog Card Number: 72-13896
© Phoebus Publishing Company/BPC Publishing
Limited, 1971/1972/1979
Filmsetting by Petty and Sons Ltd., Leeds, England.
Printed in the United States of America

4567899

All recipes have been tested either at the Cordon Bleu Cookery School in London or in our U.S. test kitchens.

Note: all recipe quantities in this book serve 4 people unless otherwise stated.

Contents

From the Editor

Greek moussaka, Egyptian falafel, Moroccan couscous — the dishes and the countries are different but a coherent style of **Middle Eastern Cooking** thrives in the area stretching from Greece around the Mediterranean to Morocco. Further north, in Sweden, Denmark, Norway and Finland, you'll also discover that the ties that bind these countries produce a unified style of **Scandinavian Cooking**. Here hearty recipes like Jansson's Temptation — potatoes baked with anchovies, onions and cream — are designed to keep out the winter cold, and the saffron, rye and raisin breads are renowned. Equally hearty are the soups, salads and side dishes that make use of **Dried Peas and Beans**.

From France came the inspiration for **Classic Entrées** like suprêmes of chicken Pascale — chicken breasts poached in stock and served on croûtes with a creamy mushroom sauce — that are ideal for elegant entertaining. And for more international favorites, you'll find a world of **Sausages** exists in Volume 12 of the Grand Diplôme Cooking Course, with Polish kielbasa, German bockwurst, French boudin blanc and many more homemade sausages. Delve into the past for **Festive Party Dishes** like roast suckling pig resplendent on a bed of rosemary branches, together with more star recipes from the London Cordon Bleu Cookery School. **Party Desserts and Cookies** include a rich chocolate mille feuilles filled with chestnuts, and fruit-topped Polish mazurki. Other ideas for entertaining appear in **Chafing Dish Cooking**, and there are **Menus** for dinners centered on stuffed pork tenderloin or a luxurious braised fillet of beef.

Don't resist temptation — Bon Appétit!

Anne Willan

SET A DANISH SMØRREBRØD TABLE

Take a break from routine and give a buffet party that requires no cooking. Let your guests create their own smørrebrød — Danish open-face sandwiches — from a tempting array of cold meats, fish, salads and a variety of breads.

Smoked Salmon	Crowded Shrimps
Eel & Egg	Egg & Caviar

Hello to Snaps

Danish Liver Pâté	Vet's Midnight Snack
Hans Christian Andersen	Salami
Roast Beef	Lion's Snack
Copenhagen Sandwich	Viking Galley

Cheese Sandwich
Savory Danish Cheesecake
Klenäter
(Swedish Christmas Crullers)

∾

Aquavit   Beer

DANISH SMØRREBRØD

In Denmark, an open-face sandwich is a smørrebrød; in Norway, it's a smørbrod; in Sweden, it's a smörgås. From the latter comes the familiar word for a buffet — a smörgåsbord. And to confuse things further, in Sweden, smörbröd refers to a French bread roll.

Scandinavians make a complete meal of these sandwiches, starting with fish, then meat and ending with cheese.

Half the charm of open-face sandwiches is their eye appeal, but this must also be equaled by their flavor. Be sure that all the ingredients are very fresh and your chosen garnishes are varied and colorful.

You can make the sandwiches ahead of time, arranging them on a huge platter and then chilling them. Otherwise, spread the table with an array of ingredients and let the guests make their favorite combinations, guiding them with a menu and descriptions of the traditional favorites like Hans Christian Andersen, Hello to Snaps and Copenhagen Sandwich.

Selection of Smørrebrød Ingredients

marinated herring
herring in sherry
homemade liver pâté
smoked salmon
raw eggs
tiny shrimps
sliced salami
black or red caviar
smoked eel
ground beef
sliced cooked ham, tongue, salted veal and rare roast beef
Camembert cheese triangles
Danish blue cheese
slices of any Scandinavian hard cheese
herring, beet and apple salad in mayonnaise
salad of cooked carrots, peas and asparagus tips in mayonnaise
apple salad
salad of cooked carrot, beets and apples in mayonnaise
sliced white, rye and pumpernickel bread

Garnishes

sliced hard-cooked egg
lemon slices
chopped chives
fried bacon slices
sliced tomato
chopped aspic
grated horseradish
canned mandarin orange sections
sliced raw or fried onion
tartare sauce
mayonnaise
butter
homemade savory pork fat
sprigs of dill

Danish Liver Pâté

1 lb calves' or pigs' liver
1½ cups milk
3 tablespoons flour
½ lb pork fat
1 teaspoon salt
½ teaspoon pepper
¼ teaspoon allspice
1 onion, quartered
2 eggs

Medium loaf pan
(8½ X 4½ X 2½ inches)

Method

Stir milk into flour and heat mixture in a saucepan, stirring, until it thickens. Simmer 1 minute, add seasonings and cool. Grind liver, pork fat and onion finely and stir into cool milk mixture with the eggs. Pour into loaf pan and bake in a moderately hot oven (375°F) for 45 minutes or until firm and brown and a skewer inserted in the center for 1 minute is hot to the touch when withdrawn. For a soft crust, bake as above, setting the pan in a water bath. Cool and slice as needed.

Unsliced pâté will keep, covered, up to 2–3 days in the refrigerator.

Savory Pork Fat
Melt 1 lb lard in a saucepan. Add 6 medium onions, peeled and finely chopped, and simmer until the onions are brown. Chill and use as needed.

Hello to Snaps

On buttered pumpernickel, arrange strips of marinated herring, herring in sherry, and salad made of chopped marinated herring, diced beets and apple in mayonnaise, seasoned with tartare sauce and colored with red food coloring; garnish with dill.

Vet's Midnight Snack

Spread pumpernickel with savory pork fat and arrange liver pâté and sliced ham on it; top with sliced tongue or salted veal and chopped aspic.

Salami

Spread pumpernickel with savory pork fat; arrange crinkled slices of salami on top.

Egg and Caviar

On buttered pumpernickel, overlap slices of hard-cooked egg, with caviar and mayonnaise arranged in strips on top.

Hans Christian Andersen

Spread buttered rye with liver pâté and top with crisp bacon and tomato slices, chopped aspic and freshly grated horseradish.

Lion's Snack

Spoon fresh uncooked ground beef on buttered pumpernickel; place an egg yolk like a flower in the middle, and arrange tiny shrimps around it.

Ingredients for smørrebrød include (from left): a selection of sliced cooked meats and fish (marinated herring, smoked salmon and shrimps), together with a dish of mandarin orange sections, salad of cooked peas, carrots and asparagus tips in mayonnaise

Have your guests choose their sandwiches from the colorful smørrebrød table (see the key on opposite page) – or let them create their own

Eel and Egg

Thoroughly beat whole eggs and pour into a shallow buttered ovenproof dish and bake in a moderate oven (350°F) for 10–15 minutes so that a smooth firm layer of egg is formed. Cool, cut in strips and arrange on pumpernickel with strips of smoked eel and apple salad; scatter with chopped chives.

Roast Beef

Place thin slices of rare beef on buttered rye with tartare sauce; top with fine slices of raw or fried onion.

Viking Galley

Overlap slices of cooked tongue on buttered pumpernickel with a salad of cooked diced carrot, diced beet and apple mixed with mayonnaise. Top salad with drained sections of mandarin orange.

Copenhagen Sandwich

Place folded slices of ham on buttered pumpernickel with a salad of cooked carrots, peas and asparagus tips, mixed with mayonnaise.

Crowded Shrimps

Overlap rows of tiny shrimps on buttered white bread; garnish with lemon slices.

Smoked Salmon

Place slices of smoked salmon on buttered white bread; decorate with slices of lemon.

Cheese Sandwich

Arrange slices of cheese and crisp bacon on buttered pumpernickel; top with triangles of Camembert.

Savory Danish Cheesecake

1 package (8 oz) cream cheese
1 package (8 oz) Danish blue cheese
1 (8 oz) rindless Camembert cheese
1 cup heavy cream, whipped until it holds a soft shape
¾ cup finely chopped walnuts
8 radishes
salt and pepper
12 triangles dark pumpernickel bread

8 inch springform pan; pastry bag and medium star tube

Serves 12 people.

Method
Soften the cheeses, work them through a sieve or food mill and beat together until thoroughly combined. Stir lightly whipped cream into cheese mixture, and reserve ¾ cup. Combine remainder with walnuts and 7 of the radishes, finely chopped. Season to taste.

In the cake pan, lay flat 6 triangles of pumpernickel, fill with cheese and walnut mixture, cover and chill overnight.

Turn cake onto a platter so pumpernickel is on top, and decorate with rosettes of reserved cheese mixture, filled into a pastry bag fitted with a star tube. Cut remaining 6 triangles in half and put 'wings' of pumpernickel around edge of cake with the remaining radish, cut into a rose, in the center.

Spoon cheese and walnut mixture onto pumpernickel triangles arranged in the pan

Cheesecake, turned out and decorated with 'wings' of pumpernickel around rosettes of the cheese mixture

SMØRREBRØD SELECTION

1 & 9	Lion's Snack
2 & 13	Copenhagen Sandwich
3 & 12	Hello to Snaps
4	Roast Beef Sandwich
5	Viking Galley
6	Smoked Salmon Sandwich
7 & 10	Salami Sandwich
8	Cheese Sandwich
11	Crowded Shrimps (see also on tray behind)
14	Hans Christian Andersen
15	Egg and Caviar Sandwich

The finished savory Danish cheesecake – an attractive and unusual end to a meal

Drinks for a Smørrebrød Party

The Scandinavian countries are among the few European states without a wine industry, so to complement their native foods – particularly the smørrebrød – they often turn to those 'home grown' alcoholic beverages that their northern climate has permitted them to produce. These include some of the world's finest beers and a unique liquor called aquavit (snaps) – 'water of life'.

Beer is the best accompaniment to a smørrebrød because of the salty flavors in so many of the toppings. While only a few of the myriad types of beer produced in Denmark, Sweden and Norway reach us, those that do are excellent. Their character is more bracing than the average lager in North America and their contribution to the success of a smørrebrød buffet will be worth the extra cost.

Aquavit is the traditional cocktail for a smørrebrød. It has no precise counterpart in our inventory of spirits, but might be compared most closely to vodka. Aquavit is a strong, usually colorless drink derived from potatoes and grain; it is flavored with spices and herbs, such as caraway, anise or fennel, and is drunk 'neat' in a single swallow without ice or mixers. Novices will do well to follow the Scandinavian practice of chilling the bottle and glasses stone cold before pouring. It is not a cocktail to linger over, but the meal's first taste sensation and a bracing accompaniment to the bold flavors of a smørrebrød.

Klenäter
(Swedish Christmas Crullers)

4 egg yolks
$\frac{1}{4}$ cup confectioners' sugar
1 tablespoon brandy
grated rind of 1 lemon
$1\frac{1}{4}$ cups flour
2 tablespoons melted butter
deep fat (for frying)
confectioners' sugar
**   (for sprinkling)**

Fluted pastry wheel

These fritters are a very simple but attractive dessert to make to complete a smørrebrød.

Method
Beat the egg yolks with the sugar until thick and light. Beat in the brandy and lemon rind, then stir in the flour with the melted butter and work lightly to form a smooth dough. Cover and chill 30 minutes.

Roll out the dough to $\frac{1}{8}$ inch thickness and cut into $\frac{3}{4}$ inch strips 3 inches long with a fluted pastry wheel. Cut a long slit in the center and twist one end through it so the strip is knotted.

Heat the deep fat to 375°F on a fat thermometer and fry the klenäter, a few at a time, until golden brown. Drain them well on paper towels and sprinkle with confectioners' sugar before serving, if you like.

Klenäter – a delicious brandy and lemon flavored fritter – may be served plain or sprinkled with confectioners' sugar

SCANDINAVIAN COOKING

The cooking of Scandinavia is greatly influenced by climate, and the harsh weather dictates which foods can be produced. Hearty meals are needed to cheer the long northern winter nights and to keep out the cold.

Fish is a universal staple. Denmark, Norway, Sweden and Finland all have long coastlines and the few areas that are far from the sea have ready access to lakes so a wide variety of fresh fish is available all year. Rich, meaty salmon is the acknowledged king, served hot or cold, smoked or pickled. One unique Scandinavian dish is gravlax — raw salmon that is marinated in salt, pepper and sugar with plenty of fresh dill for flavor; connoisseurs consider it superior to smoked salmon. Among the best freshwater fish are trout and superb crayfish that look like baby lobsters.

In many areas, fresh ingredients are severely limited during the winter months and for hundreds of years, salted, smoked, dried and pickled herring and cod sustained Scandinavians through the long winters. Today refrigeration has made a much wider range of foods available but the taste for preserved fish and meat still persists. Pickled vegetables like cucumbers, beets and onions, are popular too, and fruits, including the famous lingonberries, are canned in large quantities.

In the south the rich pastures of Denmark yield dairy products that are world renowned — butter, milk and thick cream — and also bacon and pork. In the more austere climate of the northern regions, milk, cream and butter are less plentiful but they play an important part in cooking.

Bread is a basic at Scandinavian meals — rye bread, light, dark or flavored with caraway seeds, is traditional, but Scandinavians are also expert bakers of wheat breads, rolls and a huge variety of sweet yeast breads, buns and pastries. A typical sight on Sunday morning is Pappa with the children and dog walking home from the bakery loaded down with fresh bread, rolls and pastries to eat with coffee as an evening snack around 9 p.m. A favorite way of getting together in the country is to gather in the local community house — after church or for a special celebration — to drink coffee or hot chocolate, and eat pastries and layer cake.

Bread is also the foundation of Scandinavia's popular Danish smørrebrød (see pages 8–15). Literally hundreds of different open sandwiches are offered by the famous restaurants in Copenhagen. Throughout Scandinavia, a lavish spread of cold dishes, including fish, meat and cheese, is customarily served at the beginning of a meal. A cold buffet or Danish Kolde Bord is equally popular as a complete menu of one delicacy after another, starting with the many varieties of herring, then going on to fillet of sole, shrimps, smoked eel and smoked salmon, lobster, roast beef, pork tenderloin with fried onions, frikadeller (meat balls), duckling, ham, liver pâté and all kinds of salads, ending with rich pastries.

Beer is a universal drink and few parties are complete without snaps (aquavit), the Scandinavian vodka, that should be drunk from the glass in one gulp, accompanied by the greeting 'skål'.

Fisksoppa
(Norwegian Fish Soup)

¾ lb cod or haddock
2 tablespoons butter
2 leeks, thinly sliced
2 potatoes, peeled and diced
3 carrots, peeled and diced
3 stalks of celery, thinly sliced
6 cups water
salt and pepper
1 tablespoon chopped fresh dill or parsley (for garnish)

Method
In a kettle melt butter, add vegetables and cook over low heat for 2–3 minutes until butter is absorbed. Add water, season, bring to a boil, cover and simmer 5 minutes. Add fish and continue simmering 5 minutes longer or until fish flakes easily. Take out fish, flake it, remove skin and bones, return flesh to pan and reheat. Taste soup for seasoning and sprinkle each bowl with a little chopped dill or parsley before serving.

Gravlax
(Swedish Marinated Salmon)

1½ lb fresh middle cut piece of salmon
large bunch of fresh dill
3 tablespoons coarse or kosher salt
3 tablespoons sugar
12 white peppercorns, crushed

For garnish
1 lemon, halved and notched
1 lime, halved and notched (optional)
small bunch of fresh dill

The salmon must be fresh and should be served immediately after marinating. It should be kept in the refrigerator while marinating.

Serves 6 people as an appetizer or 4 people as a main course.

Method
Scrape the salmon skin with the back of a knife to remove any scales and wipe fish with a damp cloth dipped in salt; do not wash it.

With a sharp knife, slit the piece of salmon along the backbone and cut the flesh away from the backbone in 2 pieces. Discard the backbone and any small bones.

Set 1 piece of fish, cut surface up, in a dish (not metal) and lay the dill on top. Mix the salt, sugar and crushed peppercorns and sprinkle over the dill and salmon. Set remaining piece of salmon on top, cut side down; if the thickness of the 2 salmon pieces is very uneven, turn the top one so the thick end rests on the thin end underneath and the salmon pieces are fairly flat.

Set a heavy board or a plate with a 4 lb weight on top of the salmon. Let stand in the refrigerator for 48 hours, turning the salmon every 12 hours and basting it with the liquid that will come out of the fish. Serve the salmon only after marinating it for at least 2 days.

To serve: drain the fish on paper towels and discard the seasonings and dill. Set the 2 pieces of salmon on a board, skin sides down, and cut the flesh in very thin slices with a sharp knife; arrange them on a platter. Alternatively, the salmon may be cut in serving pieces.

Garnish the platter with lemon and lime halves, if you like, and fresh dill and serve the salmon with mustard sauce and freshly ground black pepper.

The salmon can be served as a main course with poached eggs and creamed spinach or boiled potatoes as accompaniments.

To make gravlax — set one piece of salmon in a dish and lay the bunch of dill on top; sprinkle with the salt mixture

Sennepssovs
(Swedish Mustard Sauce)

2 tablespoons prepared hot mustard
1 tablespoon sugar
1 egg yolk
2 tablespoons vinegar
½ cup oil
2 tablespoons chopped dill
salt and pepper

Serve with marinated fish.

Method
Mix the mustard, sugar, egg yolk and vinegar and beat well. Beat in the oil, a little at a time, until the mixture thickens slightly, then beat in the remaining oil in a steady stream. Add the dill and season to taste — the sauce should be hot but not fiery.

Place remaining piece of salmon on top, cut side down, and set a heavy board on top

Gravlax — raw salmon is marinated in salt, pepper and sugar

Jansson's Temptation – this Swedish dish includes alternate layers of potatoes, onions and anchovies baked with cream

Janssons Frestelse
(Jansson's Temptation – Swedish)

2 large onions, thinly sliced
5 medium potatoes, cut in coarse julienne strips
16 anchovy fillets, drained and liquid reserved
3 tablespoons butter
pepper
1–1½ cups light cream

The dish is often served as a midnight snack after a dance or the theater.

Method
In a skillet melt 2 tablespoons butter; fry the onions over medium heat until soft but not browned. In a shallow buttered baking dish arrange potatoes, onions and anchovies in layers, starting and ending with potatoes; sprinkle each layer with pepper.

Pour over 1 cup of the cream, dot the top with the remaining butter and bake in a hot oven (400°F) for ¾–1 hour or until the top is golden brown and the potatoes are tender when tested with a knife. Most, but not all, of the cream should be absorbed during cooking; if dish gets dry, add more cream.

Fylld Hel Fisk
(Danish Stuffed Whole Fish)

2–2½ lb fish (striped bass or cod, or 1 whole pike – preferably not cleaned)
½ cup butter
¼ cup browned breadcrumbs
salt and pepper
1 cup light cream
1 cup white wine, or water
Danish horseradish sauce (to serve)

For stuffing
1 cucumber, seeds removed and diced
1 onion, finely chopped
2 tablespoons butter
2 cups cooked rice
3 hard-cooked eggs, chopped
3 tablespoons chopped parsley

For garnish
4 medium tomatoes
1 tablespoon butter
1 lemon, cut in wedges

Method
If you can buy fish that are not cleaned, you can then clean them by removing the entrails through the back of the fish so a large pocket is left for the filling.

Wash the fish and scrape them with the back of a knife to remove the scales. With a sharp knife slit along the backbone and down one side to the stomach, starting at the head and slitting about two-thirds of the way along the fish. Remove and discard the entrails and wash the stomach cavity thoroughly. Pat the fish dry with paper towels. Repeat with remaining fish.

To make stuffing: sprinkle the cucumber with salt, cover and let stand 30 minutes to draw out the juices (dégorger). Rinse with cold water and drain thoroughly. Cook the onion in the butter until soft

Fylld hel fish (Danish stuffed whole fish) – made here with striped bass – are ready to be baked with cream, wine, and a stuffing of rice, cucumber and hard-cooked egg

but not brown and add to the rice with cucumber, eggs, chopped parsley and plenty of seasoning.

Fill the stuffing into the fish, stuffing the cavities well and mounding the filling so the back of the fish gapes open. Set the fish in a buttered baking dish and place the ½ cup butter in thin slices along the top of each fish. Sprinkle them with the breadcrumbs and seasoning and pour the cream and wine or water into the dish.

Bake the fish in a moderate oven (350°F) for 25–30 minutes or until the fish flakes easily when tested with a fork; baste often during cooking.

To prepare garnish: halve the tomatoes, set them in a small buttered baking dish and top with the butter and seasoning. Bake in the oven with the fish for 10–15 minutes or until just cooked.

To serve, transfer the fish to a platter, arranging them diagonally on the dish. Strain the cooking liquid for the horseradish sauce. Set the tomatoes and lemon wedges around the edge of the platter and serve with peberrodssvors (Danish horseradish sauce).

Peberrodssvors
(Danish Horseradish Sauce)

2 tablespoons grated fresh horseradish or ¼ cup prepared horseradish
2 tablespoons butter
2 tablespoons flour
1½ cups liquid from cooking fish
salt and pepper

Method
In a saucepan melt the butter and stir in the flour. Pour in the fish liquid, off the heat, bring to a boil, stirring constantly, and simmer 2 minutes. Take from heat, stir in horseradish and season to taste.

Sillgratin
(Swedish Herring Pudding)

2 salt herring
2 tablespoons butter
2 onions, sliced
4 medium potatoes, sliced
pepper
½ cup melted butter
   (for serving)

For custard
2 cups milk
3 eggs, beaten to mix

This makes an attractive supper dish when cooked in individual gratin dishes instead of a large baking dish. Allow 25–30 minutes baking time instead of 50–60 minutes.

Method
Soak the fish in several changes of cold water for 8 hours. Drain fish, remove any skin and bones and cut in chunks.

In a skillet heat the butter and fry the onion over medium heat until soft but not browned. In a buttered baking dish arrange the potatoes, herring and onion in layers, starting and ending with potato and sprinkling each layer with pepper.

For custard: stir the milk into the beaten eggs and pour over the pudding. Bake the dish in a moderate oven (350°F) for 50–60 minutes or until custard is firm and the potatoes are tender.

To serve, melt the butter and, if you like, cook to a noisette (nut-brown). At once pour into a bowl and serve separately.

Kräftor
(Swedish Crayfish with Dill)

8 dozen live crayfish
4 quarts water
5 tablespoons salt
several large bunches of dill
   (reserve some for garnish)
   or 2 tablespoons dill seed

Crayfish are popular not only in Sweden but also all over Scandinavia. Traditionally a glass of snaps is tossed down after each crayfish – and each person eats 2 dozen or more.

Crayfish are found in some American rivers and are fished particularly around New Orleans and in Wisconsin, where there is a large Scandinavian population.

Method
Wash the crayfish thoroughly in cold water – it is important that they are alive before cooking.

Bring the water to a boil with the salt, add a large bunch of dill or dill seed tied in a piece of cheesecloth, and boil 5 minutes. Remove the dill, reserving it, add the live crayfish, cover the pan and bring the water back to a boil as fast as possible. Boil 5–7 minutes, depending on the size of the crayfish.

Transfer the crayfish to a large bowl, add the reserved dill, pour over the cooking liquid and let cool. If preparing in advance, keep crayfish in the liquid in refrigerator.

To serve, drain the crayfish, pile them in a bowl or on a platter and garnish with fresh dill. Serve crayfish with toast and mayonnaise. They are eaten with the fingers – a small sharp knife or scissors, and a lobster pick are best for dissecting them.

Swedish crayfish with dill – traditionally, a glass of snaps is tossed down after each crayfish

Marineret Stegt Svinekam
(Danish Marinated Roast Pork)

2½–3 lb piece of boned loin of pork or leg of fresh ham
2 tablespoons oil
salt and pepper
1 cup (¼ lb) mushrooms, sliced (optional)
½ cup heavy cream
2 teaspoons arrowroot or cornstarch (mixed to a paste with 2 tablespoons water)

For marinade
1 bottle of red wine
1 onion, sliced
2 teaspoons rosemary
4 bay leaves
1 tablespoon juniper berries
1 teaspoon black peppercorns

Throughout Scandinavia, particularly in Denmark, pork is served on special occasions.

Method
Combine all the ingredients for the marinade, place the meat in a deep dish or bowl (not metal), pour over the marinade and cover, making sure the meat is completely immersed. Refrigerate for at least 24 hours and up to 3 days, if you like.

Drain the pork and pat dry with paper towels; strain and reserve the marinade. In a flameproof casserole heat the oil and brown the pork on all sides. Pour over half the reserved marinade, sprinkle the meat with a little salt and pepper, cover the pan and bake in a moderate oven (350°F) for 1½–2 hours or until a meat thermometer inserted in the meat registers 185°F.

Set the meat on a platter and keep warm. Add the remaining marinade to the pan and boil until reduced by half and, if you like, add the mushrooms and simmer 2 minutes or until tender. Add the cream, bring just to a boil and taste for seasoning. Stir in the arrowroot or cornstarch paste and cook, stirring, just until the sauce thickens. Spoon a little of the sauce over the meat and serve the rest separately. Serve the pork with mashed potatoes.

Frikadeller
(Danish Meat Balls)

½ lb ground veal
½ lb ground pork
¼ cup fine dry white breadcrumbs
salt and pepper
2 tablespoons grated onion
½ cup light cream
½ cup water

For poaching
1 quart water
slice of onion
piece of carrot
bouquet garni
few peppercorns

Frikadeller are usually thought of as Danish but they are made, under different names, throughout Scandinavia. There are innumerable versions, some poached as in this recipe and some fried in butter over medium heat (the pan must be shaken often so the balls brown evenly). They can be made with beef, pork or veal or a mixture of all 3 meats. The same balls are also used as a garnish for beef or vegetable broth.

Method
Mix the breadcrumbs with the veal and pork. Season, add the onion and gradually stir in the cream and water. Beat the mixture until it is smooth and comes away from the sides of the bowl, then dampen your hands and roll a little of the mixture into a 1 inch ball.

In a large shallow kettle bring the water to a boil with the vegetables, bouquet garni, salt and peppercorns. Drop in the meat ball and simmer it 4–5 minutes. Drain it and taste – if meat ball is hard, work ¼ cup more water into the meat mixture. Shape the remaining balls and simmer them 4–5 minutes. Drain them and serve with mashed potatoes or boiled rice and citronsovs (lemon sauce).

Citronsovs
(Danish Lemon Sauce)

velouté sauce (made with 2 tablespoons butter 2 tablespoons flour, 1½ cups veal stock, ½ cup light cream)
juice of ½ lemon
salt and pepper

For liaison
2 egg yolks
¼ cup heavy cream

Serve with frikadeller. If the velouté sauce is made with fish stock instead of veal stock, this lemon sauce can also be served with fish.

Method
Make the velouté sauce and simmer until it is glossy and the consistency of heavy cream. Add the lemon juice and taste for seasoning. Mix the egg yolks with the cream, stir in a little hot sauce and return this mixture to the remaining sauce. Heat, stirring constantly, until the sauce thickens slightly but do not let it boil.

Labskovs
(Danish Hash)

2 cups cubed cooked meat (pork, ham or beef)
6 medium potatoes, cut in pieces
1¼–1½ cups stock
1 bay leaf
4 peppercorns
salt and pepper

For serving
3–4 tablespoons butter
1 tablespoon chopped chives or scallion tops

Method
Put meat, potatoes and 1¼ cups stock in a pan, add the bay leaf and peppercorns, tied in a piece of cheesecloth, cover and simmer 20 minutes or until potatoes are very soft and mushy. Take from heat, remove cheesecloth bag and beat or mash the mixture until potatoes are smooth, adding more stock, if necessary, so potatoes form a creamy purée. Season, and top each serving with a pat of butter and a sprinkling of chives or scallion tops. Serve the labskovs with pickled beets or cucumber.

Both the following pickle recipes are popular all over Scandinavia.

Syltede Rødbeder
(Danish Pickled Beets)

1 lb cooked whole beets, peeled
¾ cup white or cider vinegar
½ cup water
2–3 tablespoons sugar
salt and pepper
2 teaspoons caraway seed (optional)

Method
Cut large beets in slices and leave small beets whole; put them in a deep bowl (not metal).

Bring the remaining ingredients, except the caraway seed, to a boil, simmer 2 minutes and pour over the beets. Sprinkle with the caraway seed, if you like, cover and let cool.

Let stand at least 8 hours and drain before serving. The beets can be kept, covered, up to 2 weeks in refrigerator.

Syltede Agurker
(Danish Pickled Cucumber)

2 cucumbers
salt and pepper
¾ cup white or cider vinegar
¼ cup water
2 tablespoons sugar (or to taste)
1 tablespoon chopped fresh dill or parsley

Method
Peel the cucumbers if they are coated with wax; otherwise wash them thoroughly. Slice them as thinly as possible, preferably on a mandoline slicer.

Arrange slices in a bowl in layers and sprinkle each layer with salt. Cover and let stand 30 minutes to draw out the juices (dégorger), then rinse and drain thoroughly.

Mix the vinegar, water, sugar and salt and pepper and pour over the cucumber in a bowl. Cover and chill at least 2–3 hours, then drain. Sprinkle with dill or parsley before serving.

Bärsoppa
(Berry Soup)

3–4 cups blueberries, cherries or cranberries
1 quart water
2–3 tablespoons sugar (or to taste)
2 tablespoons potato starch (mixed to a paste with ¼ cup cold water)

For garnish
8 lemon slices or ½ cup heavy cream, stiffly whipped
¼ cup browned, shredded almonds

Method
Rinse and drain the berries; pick over the blueberries and cranberries and pit the cherries, removing the stems. Bring the water to a boil and add the fruit and sugar. Simmer 2–4 minutes or until the fruit is just cooked. Stir in the potato starch paste and continue cooking just until the soup thickens.

Serve the soup tepid or cold. If serving tepid, garnish each bowl with lemon slices; if serving cold, garnish with a spoonful of whipped cream and a sprinkling of browned almonds.

Fruktsoppa
(Swedish Fruit Soup)

¼ lb dried prunes
¼ lb dried apricots
6 dried apple rings
1 quart water
2 inch stick of cinnamon
grated rind and juice of ½ lemon
½ cup sugar
1 tablespoon arrowroot or potato starch (mixed to a paste with 2 tablespoons water)
1 cup heavy cream (to serve)

Dried fruit soup is served as a dessert in Norway and Finland as well as Sweden. In the far north, dried fruit soup is an important source of certain vitamins, and often the only one in the long winters.

Method
Put dried fruits in a saucepan with the water and let soak for 2 hours.

Add cinnamon stick, grated lemon rind and juice, cover, bring to a boil and simmer 15 minutes or until fruits are just tender. Stir in sugar until it dissolves; stir in arrowroot or potato starch paste and heat until the mixture thickens. Remove cinnamon stick, let cool and chill the soup thoroughly before serving with a pitcher of heavy cream.

Rødgrød med Fløde
(Danish Berry Compote with Cream)

3–4 cups red berries (strawberries, raspberries, blueberries or red currants or a mixture of any of these)
2½ cups water
¼ cup sugar (or to taste)
3 tablespoons arrowroot or potato starch (mixed to a paste with ⅓ cup water)
1 cup heavy cream, whipped until soft (to serve)

This compote is the national dessert of Denmark.

Method
Wash and drain berries, hull strawberries and pick over remaining fruit.

In a saucepan bring the water to a boil, add the fruit and sugar and simmer 5 minutes or until the fruit is soft. Cool a little, then work through a wire sieve or purée in a blender. Return the purée to the pan, bring to a boil and stir in the arrowroot or potato starch paste. As soon as the mixture thickens, take it from the heat, taste it, add more sugar, if necessary, and let cool.

Pour compote into a glass bowl; chill thoroughly. Serve with whipped cream and sugar.

The brilliant red of Danish berry compote contrasts with the bowl of whipped cream

Julglögg
(Scandinavian Hot Punch)

1 bottle of aquavit
1 bottle of red Bordeaux
10 cardamom seeds
5 whole cloves
3 strips of orange peel
2 inch piece of cinnamon stick
$\frac{1}{2}$ lb cube sugar

For serving
1 cup whole, blanched
 almonds
1 cup raisins

Serves 10–12 people.

Method
In a kettle mix aquavit, wine, cardamom seeds, cloves, orange peel and cinnamon. Bring slowly to a boil. Place sugar, a few pieces at a time, on a slotted spoon over kettle. Flame some glögg in a ladle and pour it, flaming, over sugar until it dissolves. Cover kettle and infuse for 30 minutes, but do not let the glögg boil.

Serve julglögg very hot and add a few almonds and raisins to each glass or punch mug.

Put cubes of sugar, a few at a time, in a slotted spoon and pour over flaming julglögg until they are dissolved

To make Danish raisin coffeecake in a circle, prepare double quantity of the dough, roll it into 2 rectangles and shape 2 rolls instead of 1 long one. Transfer rolls to a baking sheet and curve them into a circle. Cut them with scissors almost to the bottom at ½ inch intervals, then pull the slices alternately to one side, then to the other as shown below

BREADS AND CAKES

Flettbrød
(Danish Braided Twist)

4 cups all-purpose flour
$1\frac{1}{4}$ cups milk
$\frac{1}{2}$ cup butter
1 package dry or 1 cake
   compressed yeast
pinch of salt
2 teaspoons ground cardamom
$\frac{1}{2}$ cup sugar
1 egg
1 egg, beaten to mix with
   $\frac{1}{2}$ teaspoon salt (for glaze)
$\frac{1}{2}$ cup shredded almonds
   (for sprinkling)

Method

Heat the milk with the butter until butter is melted, cool to lukewarm and sprinkle over the yeast; let stand 5 minutes or until yeast is dissolved.

Sift the flour with the salt and cardamom into a warm bowl, stir in the sugar and make a well in the center. Pour in the yeast mixture, add the egg and mix with the hand to a dough that is soft but not sticky, adding a little more flour, if necessary. Turn out onto a floured board and knead until dough is smooth and elastic. Return to a warm greased bowl, cover it with a damp cloth and let rise in a warm place for 40–50 minutes or until doubled in bulk.

Work it lightly to knock out the air, turn out onto a floured board and divide into 3 portions. Roll each piece into a long rope, join ropes together at one end and braid them to form a plait, tucking under ends. Transfer to a greased baking sheet, cover with a cloth and let dough rise again

in a warm place for 30–35 minutes or until almost doubled in bulk. Set oven at moderately hot (375°F).

Brush the bread with egg glaze, sprinkle with almonds and bake in heated oven for 30–35 minutes or until browned and bread sounds hollow when tapped. Transfer to a wire rack to cool. Slice bread and serve with butter.

Mandelbrød
(Danish Almond Coffeecake)

Make dough for flettebrød and when it has risen once, work lightly to knock out the air; roll out to a large rectangle $\frac{1}{4}$ inch thick. Beat 1 cup prepared almond paste with $\frac{1}{4}$ cup softened butter, 1 egg and $\frac{1}{4}$ teaspoon almond extract until smooth; spread over the dough. Roll up tightly and transfer to a baking sheet. With scissors, snip roll almost to bottom at $\frac{1}{2}$ inch intervals and pull slices alternately to one side, then to the other to show circular design of filling. Let rise again and bake as for flettebrød.

Rosinbrød
(Danish Raisin Coffeecake)

Make dough for fletterbrød and when it has risen once, work lightly to knock out the air and roll out to a large rectangle $\frac{1}{4}$ inch thick. Spread with $\frac{1}{4}$ cup softened butter, sprinkle with $\frac{1}{2}-\frac{2}{3}$ cup granulated or light brown sugar, $\frac{1}{2}$ cup raisins and $\frac{1}{2}$ cup shredded almonds. Roll up and snip as for mandelbrød; let rise again and bake as for flettebrød.

A spread of breakfast breads includes Danish braided twist, 3 limpa loaves and a selection of Danish light rolls with some rolls shaped as for saffransbrod (see page 31)

Limpa
(Swedish Sweet Rye Bread)

3 cups rye flour
3 cups all-purpose flour
2 teaspoons fennel seed
2 teaspoons aniseed
2 packages dry or 2 cakes
   compressed yeast
2 cups lukewarm milk
$\frac{1}{4}$ cup molasses
$\frac{1}{4}$ cup sugar
2 teaspoons salt
grated rind of 1 orange
1 teaspoon ground cumin
1 egg, beaten with $\frac{1}{2}$ teaspoon
   salt (for glaze) – optional

Two 7 inch springform pans or 2 large loaf pans (9 X 5 X 3 inches)

In Sweden this bread is made with the rind of a bitter (Seville), not sweet, orange.

Method

Crush the fennel seed and aniseed in a mortar and pestle.

In a bowl, sprinkle the yeast over the lukewarm milk and let stand 5 minutes or until dissolved. Add the molasses, sugar, salt, orange rind, fennel, aniseed and cumin to the yeast mixture and mix the flours together. Gradually work the flours into the yeast mixture to form a smooth dough, turn out onto a floured board and knead until smooth and elastic. Replace the dough in a warm floured bowl, sprinkle a little flour on top, cover with a damp cloth and let rise in a warm place for $1-1\frac{1}{2}$ hours or until doubled in bulk. Grease pans.

Work the dough lightly to knock out the air and turn out on a generously floured board.

Shape dough into 2 round or long loaves. Or make a 'cottage' shape by placing a small ball of dough on top of a larger one. Set loaves in the greased springform pans.

Set the pans on a baking sheet, cover with a cloth and let rise in a warm place for 1 hour or until almost doubled in bulk. Set oven at moderately hot (375°F).

If you like, brush loaves with egg glaze; bake in heated oven for 40–50 minutes or until they sound hollow when tapped. Cool on a wire rack.

Grahamsbröd
(Wholewheat Bread)

2½ cups wholewheat flour
1¼–1½ cups all-purpose flour
1½ cups milk
¼ cup butter
1½ packages dry or 1½ cakes
    compressed yeast
2 tablespoons molasses
1 teaspoon salt
1 egg, beaten to mix for glaze
    (optional)

Large loaf pan (9 X 5 X 3 inches)

Method
Scald milk, add butter, pour into a large bowl; let cool to lukewarm. Sprinkle yeast on top and let stand 5 minutes or until dissolved. Stir in molasses. Add wholewheat flour and salt and stir with the hand until mixture is smooth. Add all-purpose flour a little at a time to make a dough that is soft but not sticky; knead 5–10 minutes until smooth and elastic, adding more all-purpose flour if necessary. Sprinkle top with flour, cover with a damp cloth and let rise in a warm place for 1–1½ hours or until the dough is doubled in bulk. Work lightly to knock out air, turn onto a lightly floured board and knead until smooth.

Set the oven at moderately hot (375°F) and grease the pan. Shape the dough into a loaf, set into pan, cover and let rise again in a warm place for 20–25 minutes or until almost doubled in bulk. Brush with beaten egg, if you like, and bake in heated oven for 40–45 minutes or until bread sounds hollow when tapped. Transfer to a wire rack to cool.

Rundstykke
(Danish Light Rolls)

Make the dough for flettebrød (see page 29) and when it has risen once, work lightly to knock out the air and divide it into 18–24 pieces. Shape the pieces into rolls, following any of the shapes for saffransbröd (see right).

Place them on a greased baking sheet, cover with a cloth and let rise in a warm place for 15 minutes or until almost doubled in bulk. Brush the rolls with egg glaze (1 egg, beaten to mix with ½ teaspoon salt), then bake in a hot oven (425°F) for 10–15 minutes or until rolls are browned and sound hollow when tapped.

Saffransbröd
(Christmas Saffron Buns)

pinch of saffron, infused in
    ¼ cup boiling water for
    30 minutes
2 cups milk
¾ cup butter
2 packages dry or 2 cakes
    compressed yeast
6½ cups flour
½ teaspoon salt
1 cup sugar
1 egg, beaten to mix

To finish
½ cup raisins
1 egg, beaten to mix with
    ½ teaspoon salt (for glaze)

Makes 36–40 buns.

Method
Scald the milk, stir in the butter until it melts, cool to lukewarm and sprinkle over the yeast; let stand 5 minutes until the yeast is dissolved

Sift flour with salt into a bowl and make a well in the center. Add the yeast mixture, saffron liquid, sugar and egg and mix to a soft dough. Turn out onto a floured board and knead until the dough is smooth and elastic. Return to a warm greased bowl, cover with a damp cloth and let rise in a warm place for 1 hour or until doubled in bulk. Work lightly to knock out the air, turn out onto a floured board and knead 1–2 minutes. Divide the dough into small pieces and shape buns into patterns (see illustrations), making each bun 2–3 inches across.

Transfer them to a greased baking sheet, add raisins in the center of the twists or curls and cover the buns with a cloth. Let rise in a warm place for 30–35 minutes or until almost doubled in bulk.

Set oven at hot (425°F). Brush the buns with egg glaze and bake in heated oven for 10 minutes or until golden. Transfer to a wire rack to cool.

Saffron Loaves

Make dough as for saffransbröd, let rise once and shape into 2 braided loaves (as for flettebrød, see page 29). Let rise again for 30–35 minutes, brush with beaten egg and sprinkle the tops with ½ cup whole blanched almonds, finely chopped, and ½ cup crushed sugar cubes. Bake in a hot oven (425°F) for 18–20 minutes or until the bread sounds hollow when tapped. Cut in slices and serve with butter.

Feast of St. Lucia

In Sweden, the feast of St. Lucia on December 13 is celebrated as the beginning of Christmas.

Legend has it that Lucia was a young Christian girl who was put to death under the Roman Empire; the legend spread throughout Europe to Sweden where she was pictured as a blonde maiden with a gold halo.

Today, Lucia is usually represented by the fairest girl in a family and on the feast day, her task is to carry coffee and a tray of saffron buns — attended by her sisters and brothers — to her parents. By tradition, Lucia wears a white gown and is crowned with a crown of lighted candles instead of a halo.

The custom may also date from pagan times, when a big feast was held around Christmas time to celebrate the coming of light and passing of the darkest day on December 21.

Key to different bun shapes illustrated right.

1 *Priest's locks*
2 *Boy*
3 *Golden waggon*
4 *Lucia crown*
5 *Christmas boar*
6 *Lucia cats*
7 *Seven hole twist*

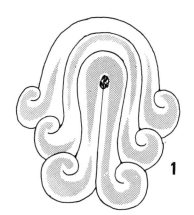

1

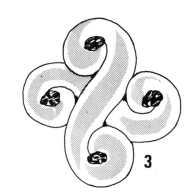

3

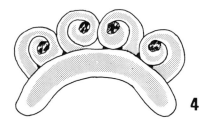

2

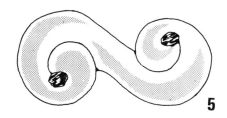

5

4

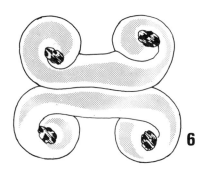

6

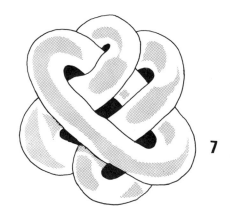

7

Escalopes of veal are garnished with thin slices of fresh orange (see page 37)

CLASSIC ENTREES (1)

Today the term entrée has come to mean any main dish, but it was originally used to describe dishes that were garnished with vegetables so that they needed no other accompaniments.

Most of these entrées are made with individual servings of meat and chicken, like lamb chops or chicken breasts, so that with a colorful garnish they are easy to arrange attractively on a platter. They are ideal dishes for formal parties — not only do they look tempting but they are easy to divide for serving. Many classic entrées like Wiener schnitzel are popular favorites; others are less widely known, although they are not hard to make.

Wiener Schnitzel

4–8 veal escalopes (about 1½ lb)
6 tablespoons clarified butter, or oil and butter, mixed (for frying)
2 lemons, halved (for garnish)
sautéed or château potatoes (for serving)

For coating
¼ cup seasoned flour (made with ¼ teaspoon salt and pinch of pepper)
1 egg, beaten with seasoning and 1 teaspoon oil)
½ cup dry white breadcrumbs

Method

Coat escalopes with seasoned flour, patting it in thoroughly. Brush with beaten egg and coat with breadcrumbs, pressing them on well.

Heat butter, or oil and butter in a large skillet and fry escalopes over medium heat for 3–4 minutes on each side until golden brown and tender. **Watchpoint**: to obtain a crisp, even coating, do not let escalopes touch each other in pan and do not move them for the first 2–3 minutes of cooking so a coating can form.

Drain escalopes thoroughly on paper towels, arrange on a platter with the sautéed or château potatoes, garnish with lemon halves and serve at once while escalopes are still crisp.

Note: the classic Wiener schnitzel is garnished only with lemon, but many chefs like to add one of the following garnishes:

1 On each escalope place a lemon slice, and top the slices with crossed anchovy fillets.

2 On each escalope place a lemon slice topped with a green olive with an anchovy fillet wrapped around it.

3 On each escalope place a lemon slice, topped with chopped capers and gherkin pickles and sprinkle with chopped parsley.

At each end of the serving platter place bands of finely chopped egg white, sieved egg yolks and chopped parsley and top the bands with a lattice of anchovy fillets.

To Flatten Escalopes

If necessary trim any skin and membrane from the veal. Lay escalopes (they are best cut from the round) between 2 sheets of wax paper and pound well with a cutlet bat or mallet to flatten them to ¼ inch thickness. If the meat is correctly prepared by the butcher, this should not be necessary.

Chicken breasts (suprêmes) are sometimes flattened in the same way.

Escalopes of Veal Italienne

4–8 veal escalopes (about 1½ lb)
¼ cup clarified butter, or oil and butter, mixed (for frying)
1 onion, finely chopped
¼ cup Marsala or sherry
1 tablespoon flour
1½ cups stock
1½ teaspoons tomato paste
1 bay leaf
salt and pepper

For garnish
1½ lb fresh or 2 packages frozen spinach
1 tablespoon butter
2 tomatoes, peeled and sliced
1 clove of garlic, crushed
5–6 tablespoons heavy cream
4 large slices of Gruyère cheese

Method

In a skillet heat the butter, or oil and butter, sauté escalopes quickly, about 1–2 minutes on each side until golden brown and remove. Add the onion and cook until soft. Replace escalopes, pour over Marsala or sherry and flame. Take out the escalopes again, boil liquid to reduce slightly, then stir in flour and add stock, tomato paste, bay leaf and seasoning. Bring to a boil, stirring, put back escalopes, cover and simmer gently for 7–10 minutes or until tender.

To prepare the garnish: cook fresh spinach in plenty of boiling salted water for 5 minutes or until just tender; cook the frozen spinach according to package directions. Drain well, pressing between 2 plates to remove excess water.

Melt butter in a frying pan, add tomatoes with garlic and seasoning and sauté briskly for 1–2 minutes or until just cooked.

Put the spinach in a pan with cream, reheat well, stirring, and arrange down center of a long ovenproof platter.

Drain the escalopes, arrange them, overlapping, on top of the spinach, with a slice of cheese (halving slices if escalopes are small) and 1–2 tomato slices on top of each escalope and brown under the broiler. Reheat sauce, strain, pour a little around the dish and serve the rest separately.

Lay the cooked escalopes on a bed of spinach before adding cheese and sautéed tomatoes

Brown escalopes of veal Italienne under broiler with tomato and cheese slices on top

Veal escalopes, arranged on croûtes, are garnished with olives stuffed with maître d'hôtel butter, and watercress

Veal Escalopes with Olives

8 small veal escalopes
   (about 1½ lb)
6 tablespoons clarified butter,
   or oil and butter, mixed
   (for frying)

For coating
¼ cup seasoned flour (made
   with ¼ teaspoon salt and
   pinch of pepper)
1 egg, beaten with seasoning
   and 1 teaspoon oil
½ cup dry white breadcrumbs

For garnish
8 large ripe olives, pitted
maître d'hôtel butter, made
   with 2 tablespoons butter,
   1 teaspoon chopped parsley,
   few drops of lemon juice, salt
   and pepper
eight 1-inch rounds of white
   bread, fried in 2–3
   tablespoons oil and butter,
   mixed, and drained
   (for croûtes)
bunch of watercress

*Pastry bag and small star tube
(optional)*

Method

To prepare garnish: cut the base off olives so they will sit upright. Fill cavity with maître d'hôtel butter, using a pastry bag and star tube, if you like. Fry the croûtes and keep warm.

Coat the escalopes with seasoned flour, patting it in thoroughly. Brush them with beaten egg and coat with breadcrumbs, pressing them on well.

Heat clarified butter, or oil and butter, in a large skillet and fry escalopes over medium heat for 3–4 minutes on each side or until golden brown and tender.

Watchpoint: to obtain a crisp, even coating, do not let escalopes touch each other in the pan and do not move them for the first 2–3 minutes of cooking so a coating can form.

Drain escalopes thoroughly on paper towels, arrange on a platter and top with croûtes. Sprinkle croûtes with chopped parsley, set an olive in the center of each one, garnish the platter with watercress and serve with Parisienne potatoes (see page 40).

Escalopes of Veal with Orange

4–8 veal escalopes (about
   1½ lb)
3 navel oranges
6 tablespoons clarified butter,
   or oil and butter, mixed
   (for frying)
1 tablespoon flour
1 tablespoon brandy or
   2 tablespoons sherry
1 cup stock
salt and pepper

Method

Grate rind and squeeze the juice from 1½ oranges. In a large skillet heat butter or butter and oil and sauté escalopes quickly, for about 1–2 minutes on each side until golden brown. Remove and reserve. Stir the flour into pan, add grated orange rind and strained orange juice with brandy or sherry and stock. Bring to a boil, stirring, replace escalopes, season, cover and simmer for 10 minutes.

Meanwhile peel the remaining oranges, cutting away all white pith with a serrated-edge knife; slice flesh thinly into rounds.

Arrange escalopes on a platter, spoon over sauce from pan and garnish with orange slices.

Veal Chops Hongroise

4 veal chops
¼ cup seasoned flour (made
   with ¼ teaspoon salt and
   pinch of pepper)
2 tablespoons olive oil
1 teaspoon paprika
½ cup Marsala or sherry
½–¾ cup well-flavored stock

For salpicon
1 eggplant
¼ cup olive oil
2 onions, finely sliced
1½ teaspoons paprika
3 slices of canned pimiento,
   drained, cut in strips and
   juice reserved
salt and pepper

Method

Coat veal chops with seasoned flour. Heat oil in a skillet and brown chops on both sides. Reduce heat, stir in paprika and cook 1 minute. Pour in Marsala or sherry and boil until reduced to almost nothing. Add ½ cup stock, cover and simmer gently for ¾–1 hour or until chops are tender and coated with a sticky glaze. Add more stock during cooking if pan is dry.

To prepare salpicon: slice eggplant, sprinkle with salt; leave for 30 minutes to draw out juices (dégorger). Rinse the slices in cold water and dry on paper towels.

Heat oil in a frying pan and brown the slices on both sides. Take out, add the onion with a little more oil if needed and brown also. Stir in paprika and pimiento, put back eggplant slices, spoon over a little reserved pimiento juice, season, cover and cook gently for 8–10 minutes or until tender.

Transfer the salpicon to a platter and arrange veal chops, overlapping, on top or serve them separately.

Lamb Chops with Walnuts

8 rib lamb chops
2 tablespoons clarified butter
salt and pepper
1 onion, thinly sliced
2 green peppers, cored,
   seeded and thinly sliced
½ cup coarsely chopped
   walnuts
½ cup white wine

Method

Trim fat and meat from bones to expose 1 inch of bone; scrape bone ends clean.

In a large heavy skillet, heat the butter and when foaming add the chops. Fry for 2–3 minutes on each side or until brown. Season after browning one side. Arrange them in a circle with the bones slanting up the platter and keep warm.

Add onion to pan, cook 2–3 minutes until it starts to brown and stir in peppers and walnuts. Cook, stirring gently, for 1–2 minutes or until very hot. Pile in the center of the platter. (Peppers should be cooked but still slightly crisp.) Add wine to pan and bring to a boil to dissolve the juices. Pour around the platter.

To clarify butter: cut regular butter into medium-sized pieces and melt in a thick saucepan over low heat. Continue to cook until foaming well, pour into a bowl and leave to settle.

Skim any foam from the top and chill; the clarified butter will form a solid cake on top. Discard liquid beneath. If not to be used at once, melt it down, pour into a covered container and store in the refrigerator.

Lamb Chops with Cheese

8 rib lamb chops
$\frac{1}{4}$ cup melted butter
$\frac{1}{2}$ cup finely grated Gruyère
    cheese
$\frac{1}{2}$ cup fresh white breadcrumbs
$1\frac{1}{2}$ lb fresh spinach or
    2 packages frozen spinach
2 tablespoons clarified butter
    (see box on page 37) or
    2 tablespoons oil (for frying)
1 tablespoon butter

For sauce
1 onion, finely chopped
$1\frac{1}{2}$ tablespoons butter
2 teaspoons flour
1 can (8 oz) tomatoes
2 slices of canned pimiento,
    drained and chopped
pinch of ground mace
bouquet garni
2 strips of lemon rind
1 teaspoon tomato paste
$\frac{3}{4}$ cup stock
salt and pepper
pinch of sugar, or to taste

Method
Trim the fat and meat from the ends of the chops to expose about 1 inch of the bone, then scrape bone ends clean. Dip chops in melted butter, then into a mixture of grated cheese and breadcrumbs, pressing them on well. Repeat the process so each chop is coated twice.

To make the sauce: cook the onion in the butter until soft. Stir in the flour, then add the remaining ingredients with seasoning and sugar to taste. Simmer the sauce 25–30 minutes until it is well reduced and full of flavor. Work it through a strainer, return it to the pan and continue to simmer until it is glossy and thickened. Taste for seasoning.

Wash fresh spinach thoroughly, remove the stems and cook it in boiling salted water for 5–6 minutes or cook frozen spinach according to package directions. Drain the spinach and press between 2 plates to remove all the water.

In a skillet heat the clarified butter or oil and fry the chops for 2–3 minutes on each side or until brown. Toss the spinach over high heat with the tablespoon of butter. Spoon a little sauce into a serving dish to coat the bottom, pile the spinach in the center of the dish. Arrange the chops around it, overlapping, with the bones pointing up. Serve the remaining sauce separately.

Lamb Chops Niçoise

8 rib lamb chops
1 clove of garlic, peeled and cut
    in half
3 tablespoons oil or clarified
    butter
$\frac{3}{4}$ cup stock, wine or water
1 teaspoon tomato paste

For garnish
1 medium eggplant, sliced
3–4 zucchini, sliced
1 large green pepper, cored,
    seeded and cut in strips
2 tomatoes, peeled, seeded
    and cut in strips
2 tablespoons olive oil
1 clove of garlic, crushed
salt and pepper

Method
Trim fat and meat from the ends of the chop bones to expose about 1 inch of the bone, then scrape bone ends clean. Rub meat with the cut side of the clove of garlic and set aside.

To prepare garnish: sprinkle the eggplant and zucchini slices with salt and leave 30 minutes to draw out the juices (dégorger). Rinse in cold water, drain and dry on paper towels. Heat half the oil in a skillet, add the eggplant slices and sauté until soft. Take out, add zucchini with the remaining oil and cook until soft. Put back the eggplant with the green pepper, tomatoes and garlic, season and cook gently, stirring occasionally, for 15 minutes or until all the vegetables are soft. Arrange on one side of the platter and keep warm.

To cook chops: heat oil or clarified butter and fry the chops for 2–3 minutes on each side or until brown. Season them after browning one side. Take from the pan, arrange, bones slanting up, on one side of the vegetable garnish and keep warm.

Discard fat from pan and dissolve the meat juices left in the pan with stock, wine or water. Stir in tomato paste, simmer 1 minute and pour this sauce around the chops.

For garnish for lamb chops Niçoise slice eggplant and zucchini, peel the tomatoes, and core and seed green pepper before cooking meat

Lamb chops Niçoise are served on a platter with mixed vegetables — eggplant, green peppers, zucchini and tomatoes

Noisettes of Lamb Louisette

2½–3 lb rack of lamb
salt and pepper
¼ cup oil (for frying)
5 tablespoons sherry

For salpicon
2 cucumbers, peeled, seeded and cut in strips
2 tablespoons butter
1 small onion, finely chopped
1 cup (¼ lb) cooked lean ham, cut in strips
2 teaspoons finely chopped fresh mint
2 tablespoons light cream (optional)

Method
Bone the lamb or ask your butcher to do it for you. Season cut surface, roll up, tie at 1–1½ inch intervals and cut into noisettes.

To prepare salpicon: blanch cucumber in boiling salted water 1 minute, drain, refresh and dry on paper towels. In a skillet melt butter and fry onion until soft but not brown. Add cucumber, ham, mint and salt and pepper. Reheat the salpicon and keep warm.

In a large skillet heat oil and fry noisettes 5–6 minutes on each side or until a light golden brown. Season after frying one side.

Watchpoint: if noisettes are browned but not sufficiently cooked to your taste (the juice that runs out when you prick them with a fork should be pink for medium done or clear for well done), set them on a rack over the skillet and bake them in a hot oven (425°F) for 4–5 minutes to complete cooking.

Arrange noisettes, overlapping, down one side of a hot platter and keep warm.

Pour off fat from pan, add sherry and deglaze meat juices left in pan. Bring to a boil and pour over noisettes. Add cream to salpicon, heat thoroughly and pile down the other side of the platter.

Noisettes are boned loin or rib chops cut from a rack of lamb. Your butcher will prepare them for you or you can make them yourself at home.

To make noisettes: remove the chop bones, using a small sharp knife and working in short, sharp strokes. Keep knife close to the bone to avoid cutting into the meat.

Season the cut surface of meat and roll it up, starting at the lean side. Trim fat if there is more than enough to wrap once around the lean meat. Tie the roll securely at 1–1½ inch intervals with fine string. Then cut between each tied section to make a 'noisette' or nut.

Depending on the size of the animal, a rack of lamb weighs from 1½–3 lb and makes enough noisettes for 2–4 people. Allow 1–2 noisettes per person.

Cut between the tied sections to make a noisette of lamb from a rack of lamb

---

Rack of Lamb Provençale

2½–3 lb rack of lamb
2 cloves of garlic, peeled and cut in slivers
1 teaspoon rosemary
1 teaspoon thyme
2–3 tablespoons olive oil
salt and pepper
½ cup white wine
½ cup stock

For garnish
4 tomatoes, cored
olive oil (for brushing)
Parisienne potatoes

Method
Trim ends of bones to expose them. Make incisions in the lamb with the point of a knife and insert slivers of garlic. Heat the oil in a roasting pan, put in the lamb, baste and sprinkle with herbs and salt and pepper. Roast, basting often, in a moderately hot oven (375°F) for 1¼ hours or until a meat thermometer inserted in the meat registers 170°F (for medium done lamb).

Set the tomatoes in a baking dish, stem sides down, brush them with oil and sprinkle them with seasoning. Bake them in the oven with the lamb for 15–20 minutes or until they are just tender. Heat 2–3 skewers in a flame or on a burner until red hot and mark a lattice on top of the tomatoes to decorate them.

To serve: transfer the lamb to a platter, arrange the tomatoes and Parisienne potatoes around it, decorate chop bones with paper chop frills, if you like, and keep warm. Discard any fat from the roasting pan and deglaze the pan juices with the wine and stock. Bring to a boil, simmer 1–2 minutes, strain, taste for seasoning and serve this gravy separately.

Parisienne Potatoes

Scoop out potato balls with a ball cutter and either boil them in salted water and toss in melted butter or sauté them in butter until tender.

Sprinkle potato balls with chopped parsley and a little salt and serve.

To Make Chop Frills

Fold a 10′ X 3 inch sheet of plain white paper in half lengthwise. With scissors make a series of even cuts ⅛ inch apart to within ¾ inch of the unfolded long edges and turn the paper inside out so the cut part is looped. Stick the two long edges together with glue and cut to make 4 frills. Fold each in a circle and attach the ends to complete the chop frill.

Rack of lamb Provençale is garnished with broiled tomatoes and Parisienne potatoes

Rack of Lamb Conti

$2\frac{1}{2}$–3 lb rack of lamb
8 anchovy fillets
1 tablespoon chopped mixed herbs (parsley, marjoram, thyme)
1 shallot, finely chopped
2–3 tablespoons oil

For garnish
1 cup dried fava or navy beans, soaked overnight and drained
salt
2 tablespoons butter
black pepper, freshly ground
1 teaspoon sugar
3 tomatoes, peeled and thickly sliced
anchovy fillets (for garnish) – optional

Larding needle

Method
Cut anchovy fillets in half lengthwise, roll them in some of the chopped herbs and shallot, reserving the rest, and lard the meat with them.

Heat oil in a roasting pan, put in the lamb, baste and roast, basting often, in a moderately hot oven (375°F) for $1\frac{1}{4}$ hours or until a meat thermometer registers 170°F (for medium done lamb).

To prepare garnish: simmer beans, covered, in water for 1–$1\frac{1}{2}$ hours for fava beans or $2\frac{1}{2}$–3 hours for navy beans, or until tender, adding salt, halfway through cooking. Drain, return beans to the pan with 1 tablespoon butter, season and keep warm.

Melt the remaining butter in a skillet and add sugar and seasoning. When hot add the tomato slices and cook quickly for 1–2 minutes on each side until brown and caramelized. Take from heat and sprinkle with reserved herbs and shallot.

Carve the lamb into chops and arrange down one side of a platter. Pile the beans on the other side and arrange the tomatoes, overlapping, on top. If you like, garnish the dish with more anchovy fillets. Serve with a gravy made from the pan juices or with Provençale sauce.

Provençale Sauce

1 cup ($\frac{1}{4}$ lb) mushrooms
$1\frac{1}{2}$ tablespoons oil
3 shallots, finely chopped
1 clove of garlic, crushed
1 tablespoon flour
$\frac{3}{4}$ cup well-flavored stock
$\frac{3}{4}$ cup white wine
salt and pepper
bouquet garni
2 teaspoons tomato paste

Method
Trim the mushroom stems level with the caps, chop the stems finely and slice the caps.

Heat the oil, add mushroom stems, shallot and garlic and cook gently for 4–5 minutes or until the shallot just begins to brown. Add the flour, pour in the stock and wine and bring to a boil, stirring. Season, add bouquet garni, simmer 20 minutes and strain. Add the tomato paste and sliced mushroom caps, bring to a boil and simmer 2–3 minutes or until mushrooms are tender.

Fillet Steak Papillon

4 thick or 8 thin fillet steaks
2 tablespoons oil (for frying)

For garnish
8 large mushrooms
2 tablespoons butter
Parisienne potatoes or château potatoes

For sauce
1 tablespoon butter
2 shallots, finely chopped
3 large mushrooms, finely chopped
2 teaspoons chopped mixed herbs (parsley, chives, tarragon)
$\frac{1}{2}$ cup white wine
1 teaspoon flour
$\frac{3}{4}$ cup stock
salt and pepper

Method
To make garnish: trim mushroom stems level with the caps; fry the caps gently in the butter until tender and keep warm. Chop stems.

To prepare the sauce: melt butter and sauté shallots with chopped mushrooms and mushroom stems until soft. Add herbs and wine, boil to reduce a little and reserve.

To cook steaks: heat oil in a large skillet and fry thick steaks over high heat for 3 minutes on each side for rare steaks, or for 1 minute only on each side if they are thin. Season them after frying one side. Arrange them, overlapping, down one side of a platter with 1–2 large mushrooms between each steak.

Discard fat from skillet, stir in flour and pour on stock. Bring to a boil, stirring to deglaze meat juices left in pan, and strain into mushroom and shallot mixture. Season, simmer 1 minute and pour over steaks.

Pile Parisienne or château

potatoes down the other side of the platter and serve.

Strip Steak Périnette

4 strip steaks, cut 1 inch thick
1–2 tablespoons oil or clarified butter (see page 37) – (for frying)

For tomato salpicon
3 tomatoes, peeled, seeded and cut in strips
1 teaspoon tomato paste
3–4 leeks, thoroughly washed
2 tablespoons butter
1 teaspoon paprika
2 red bell peppers, cored, seeded and cut in strips, or 2–3 slices of canned pimiento, drained and cut in strips
salt and pepper

Method
For salpicon: cut white part of leeks into thin rounds and the green into strips; blanch the strips and reserve. Cook the white part of the leeks in the butter until soft and add tomato paste, paprika, tomatoes and red pepper or pimiento. Season well, cover and cook 3–4 minutes until the peppers and tomatoes are just soft. Keep warm.

Broil or pan fry the steaks, and season after browning one side. Arrange them, overlapping, down one side of a platter and pile the salpicon down the other. Scatter the strips of green leek over the steak and serve.

Breasts of Chicken Maintenon

4 boned chicken breasts
$\frac{1}{4}$ cup seasoned flour (made with $\frac{1}{4}$ teaspoon salt and pinch of pepper)
$\frac{1}{2}$ cup butter
2 shallots, finely chopped
2 teaspoons flour
2 teaspoons tomato paste
$\frac{1}{2}$ cup sherry
$\frac{3}{4}$ cup stock
salt and pepper
Parisienne potatoes (for garnish)

For salpicon
1 cup ($\frac{1}{4}$ lb) mushrooms, sliced
2 tablespoons butter
2 shallots, finely chopped
1 tablespoon flour
$\frac{1}{4}$ cup stock
2 tablespoons sherry
$\frac{1}{2}$ cup ($\frac{1}{4}$ lb) cooked ham, cut in strips

For mornay sauce
2 tablespoons butter
2 tablespoons flour
1$\frac{1}{2}$ cups milk
$\frac{3}{4}$ cup grated cheese, preferably half Parmesan, half Gruyère

Method

Make the mornay sauce, using $\frac{1}{2}$ cup of cheese, and reserve.

Place the chicken breasts between 2 sheets of wax paper and pound until they are $\frac{1}{4}$ inch thick and look like veal escalopes. Coat them in seasoned flour. In a large skillet melt 6 tablespoons butter and sauté chicken pieces for 5–6 minutes on each side or until golden brown and tender.

Meanwhile prepare salpicon: melt the 2 tablespoons butter and sauté mushrooms and shallot until soft; stir in the flour, add the stock, season, and cook 1–2 minutes. Add the sherry and

ham and heat thoroughly.

Take chicken from the pan and keep warm. Add shallot to the pan and cook until soft. Stir in the flour, cook until straw-colored, then stir in the tomato paste, sherry and stock. Bring sauce to a boil, season and simmer 2–3 minutes. Strain sauce and keep hot.

Arrange the chicken on a heatproof platter and cover each piece with salpicon. Heat the mornay sauce, spoon over the chicken, sprinkle with remaining grated cheese and dot with remaining 2 tablespoons butter. Brown in a very hot oven (450°F) or under the broiler.

Watchpoint: this dish can be prepared ahead of time, then baked in a moderately hot oven (375°F) for 10–15 minutes or until browned. If necessary, finish browning under the broiler.

Garnish with Parisienne potatoes and pour sauce around.

Suprêmes of Chicken Pascale

4 suprêmes of chicken or boned chicken breasts
2–3 cups chicken stock, preferably made with chicken giblets (except liver) or chicken bones with root vegetables, bouquet garni and seasoning (for poaching)
2 cups ($\frac{1}{2}$ lb) mushrooms
1 tablespoon water
juice of $\frac{1}{2}$ lemon
béchamel sauce, made with 3 tablespoons butter, 3 tablespoons flour, 2 cups milk (infused with slice of onion, 6 peppercorns, blade of mace, and bay leaf)
small pinch of cayenne
small can (4 oz) pâté de foie gras, or any soft creamy liver pâté
salt and pepper
2 tablespoons brandy
Parisienne potatoes (for garnish)

For croûtes
4 slices of white bread, crusts removed
$\frac{1}{4}$ cup oil and butter, mixed

For butter sauce
3 tablespoons butter
1 egg yolk
1 tablespoon water

Method

Set chicken pieces in a baking dish, pour over the stock, cover with foil and poach in a moderate oven (350°F) for 25–30 minutes or until tender.

Trim mushroom stalks level with the caps and cook the caps, covered, with the water and lemon juice for 2 minutes or until just tender. Drain them, reserving the juice. Keep 8 mushroom caps, finely chop the rest and add to the béchamel sauce with the cayenne. Whisk in 1 teaspoon of the pâté and keep sauce hot in a water bath.

Cut the slices of bread in large diamond shapes, fry in oil and butter until golden and drain well. Spread them with the remaining pâté and arrange in a hot ovenproof dish. Drain the chicken pieces, remove any skin, set on the croûtes, cover and keep warm.

To prepare the butter sauce: beat egg yolk with water in the top of a double boiler over low heat until light and thick enough to leave a ribbon trail when the beater is lifted; beat in the butter a little at a time.

Slowly beat the mushroom and béchamel mixture into the butter sauce, add the reserved mushroom liquid and taste for seasoning. Spoon the sauce over the chicken and broil under a heated broiler for 1 minute or until glazed and lightly brown. Warm the brandy and spoon over the dish. Place 2 mushroom caps on each piece of chicken and spoon the Parisienne potatoes between them.

A **suprême** is all the white meat on the breast down to the wing bone on a chicken. It should be removed in one piece from the bones on each side.

Cut suprêmes down from top of breastbone with a sharp knife; keep knife close to rib cage. Detach white meat in one piece, with wing bone

Stuffed pork tenderloin — slice for serving and spoon over a little of the sauce (recipe is on page 48)

A white wine is particularly welcome with either pork or sole and both wines suggested here are aromatic although they have quite different characteristics. The dry, almost severe whites raised at the great vineyards of the Graves district of Bordeaux are most frequently served with fish. However, their special qualities, derived from the sémillon and sauvignon blanc grapes, make them more than suitable for both these entrées. For those who want a similarly exotic bouquet but have a sweet tooth, there is the Diamond, one of the best of the traditional white wines from New York State. Used chiefly as a component in the best New York sparkling wines, it is also bottled as a still, varietal type and, when served well chilled, is pleasantly refreshing.

CHOOSE SAVORY PORK OR CLASSIC SOLE

Tomato & Avocado Salad
or
Mushrooms Philippe

Stuffed Pork Tenderloin
Savoyarde Potatoes
or
Sole Bonne Femme
'Fish' Potatoes

Dacquoise

White wine — Graves (Bordeaux)
or Diamond (New York)

TIMETABLE

Day before
Soak apricots if necessary. Make meringues for dacquoise and store in airtight container.
Make breadcrumbs for pork stuffing.
Make dressing for salad.

Morning
Prepare tomatoes and chill. *Prepare the mushrooms Philippe, cover them and refrigerate.*
Cook apricots and sieve or purée; make lemon syrup for sauce.
Make stuffing, cool thoroughly and layer pork; prepare for roasting and refrigerate.
Make Hollandaise sauce for fish, cover and keep at room temperature.
Prepare Brussels sprouts or broccoli and refrigerate.
Peel potatoes (*shape for 'fish' potatoes*), and keep in cold water.
Slice and cook mushrooms for sole; cover and chill.
Wash and dry sole and place in dish ready for poaching; refrigerate.

Assemble ingredients for final cooking from 5:30 for dinner around 8 p.m.

You will find that **cooking times** given in the individual recipes for these dishes have sometimes been adapted in the timetable to help you when cooking and serving this menu as a party meal.

Order of Work

5:30
Set oven at moderate (350°F).
5:45
Brown pork; put in oven.
6:45
Slice potatoes for Savoyarde potatoes and arrange in dish. Add stock and put in oven on top shelf.
Whip cream, flavor with apricot purée and sandwich meringues together. Decorate dacquoise, place on platter; refrigerate. Dilute apricot purée with lemon syrup, pour into sauce boat and refrigerate.
7:15
Set oven at moderate (350°F) for sole. Cook 'fish' potatoes.
7:30
Put sole to cook. Drain 'fish' potatoes; dry and keep warm.
Cook Brussels sprouts or broccoli and refresh.
Peel and dice avocados, mix with dressing, fill tomatoes and chill.
7:45
Remove pork from oven and transfer to serving platter; slice and keep warm. Make gravy. Turn down oven and keep Savoyarde potatoes hot.
Drain sole; make white wine sauce; reheat mushrooms. Assemble sole dish.
8:00
Serve appetizer.
Lightly brown sole under broiler before serving.
Reheat Brussels sprouts or broccoli in butter just before serving.

Tomato and Avocado Salad

8 medium, even-sized tomatoes
2 ripe avocados
juice of ½ lemon
salt and pepper
dash of Tabasco
4—5 tablespoons vinaigrette dressing
bunch of watercress (for garnish)

Method
Scald and peel the tomatoes; cut a slice from the bottom (not stem end) of each tomato, reserving the slices. Carefully scoop out the seeds and discard. Season the insides well with lemon juice, salt, pepper and Tabasco. Chill.

Halve avocados with a silver or stainless steel knife and discard the seeds. Peel and dice the flesh, sprinkle with salt and pepper and mix with a little vinaigrette dressing.

With a teaspoon, fill tomatoes with avocado, replace lids, arrange tomatoes on individual plates and spoon over remaining dressing. Garnish with a few sprigs of watercress.

Watchpoint: do not prepare avocados more than 1 hour before serving as they will discolor.

Mushrooms Philippe

2 cups (½ lb) mushrooms
2 tablespoons olive oil
2 shallots, finely chopped
½ cup red wine
1 teaspoon thyme
2—3 tablespoons vinaigrette dressing (made with red wine vinegar)
salt and pepper

Method
Wipe the mushrooms with a damp cloth and trim each stem level with the base of the cap. Slice stems lengthwise.

Heat oil in a small skillet, add mushroom caps, the sliced stems and shallot and fry briskly, stirring for 2—3 minutes or until mushrooms are tender. Lift out with a slotted spoon and arrange in a serving dish.

Add wine to pan and boil until it is reduced by half. Add thyme and vinaigrette dressing, season well and pour over mushrooms; cover. Chill for at least 45 minutes before serving on individual plates.

Vinaigrette Dressing
For ½ cup of dressing: mix 2 tablespoons vinegar (any of the following types: red or white wine, cider or tarragon) with ½ teaspoon salt and ½ teaspoon freshly ground black pepper. Gradually add 6 tablespoons oil, preferably olive or peanut, whisking until dressing thickens slightly. Taste for seasoning.

Entrée

Stuffed Pork Tenderloin

3 pork tenderloins (about 2 lb)
2 tablespoons butter
¼ cup sherry
1 tablespoon flour
1½ cups stock
salt and pepper

For stuffing
½ lb ground veal
1 medium onion,
    finely chopped
¼ cup butter
1 tablespoon chopped parsley
1 teaspoon mixed herbs
    (thyme, basil)
1 teaspoon sage
grated rind and juice of
    ½ lemon
1 cup fresh white breadcrumbs
1 egg, beaten to mix

Method

Split the pork tenderloins lenthwise two-thirds of the way through. Open them up so they are flat, put between 2 sheets of wax paper and pound each with a mallet or rolling pin to ½ inch thickness.

Set oven at moderate (350°F).

To make the stuffing: cook onion in butter until soft but not brown, add to the remaining ingredients in a bowl, season and stir in enough beaten egg to bind the mixture. Layer stuffing between each split tenderloin and shape the meat into a loaf; tie it with string at 1½ inch intervals or fasten with skewers.

Heat butter in a flameproof casserole and brown the pork on all sides. Pour over sherry, cover securely with foil and lid and bake in heated oven for 1½–2 hours or until the pork is very tender.

Remove pork from oven and transfer to a platter; keep warm.

To prepare gravy: stir flour into pan juices and cook over low heat to a rich brown. Add stock and cook over low heat, stirring constantly, until it comes to a boil. Season, simmer 2–3 minutes and strain.

Remove string or skewers from pork, slice it and arrange on the hot platter. Spoon a little gravy around meat and serve the rest separately.

Brussels sprouts or broccoli and Savoyarde potatoes are good accompaniments to the stuffed pork tenderloin.

Accompaniment to entrée

Savoyarde Potatoes

1½ lb potatoes
1 tablespoon butter
1 clove of garlic, crushed with
    ½ teaspoon salt
salt
black pepper, freshly ground
½ cup grated Gruyère cheese
1½–2 cups stock

Mandoline slicer (optional)

Method

Set oven at moderately hot (375°F).

Peel the potatoes and cut them in thin slices, about one-eighth inch thick using a mandoline slicer, if you like. Rub an ovenproof dish with the butter and spread crushed garlic over the bottom of the dish. Arrange the potato slices in the dish, sprinkling the layers with salt, pepper and half the cheese; arrange top

Layer veal stuffing between the split pork tenderloins and shape the meat into a loaf

Brown tied pork on all sides in butter in a casserole and pour over the sherry

layer of potatoes in a neat pattern.

Pour enough stock down the side of the dish to come almost level with the top layer of potatoes. Sprinkle top with remaining cheese. Bake in heated oven for 1–1¼ hours or until potatoes are tender when tested with a skewer. The top should be golden brown.

Alternative entrée

Sole Bonne Femme

4 large or 8 small fillets of sole
6 peppercorns
slice of onion
1 bay leaf
¾ cup white wine
¾ cup water
1 cup (¼ lb) sliced mushrooms
juice of ½ lemon
salt and pepper

For Hollandaise sauce
3 tablespoons tarragon vinegar
    (seasoned with slice of
    onion, 3 peppercorns, blade
    of mace and ½ bay leaf)
2 egg yolks, beaten to mix
½ cup unsalted butter, at room
    temperature

For white wine sauce
3 tablespoons butter
2 tablespoons flour
1½ cups fish stock (from
    poaching fish)
½ cup light cream

Method

To make Hollandaise sauce boil the vinegar with its seasonings over low heat until it is reduced to 2 teaspoons. Set vinegar aside. With a wooden spoon, beat the egg yolks in a bowl with 1 teaspoon butter and a pinch of salt until light and slightly thick. Strain on the vinegar. Stand bowl in a pan of hot water or over bottom of a double boiler. Add the rest of the butter in small pieces beating hard between each addition until sauce is thick. Season, cover and reserve.

Set oven at moderate (350°F).

To prepare sole: rinse under

cold water and pat dry with paper towels. Fold fillets in half and put in a buttered ovenproof dish. Add peppercorns, onion and bay leaf and pour over the wine and water. Cover with foil and poach in heated oven for 12–15 minutes or until fish flakes easily when tested with a fork. Strain the liquid from fish and measure it – there should be $1\frac{1}{2}$ cups. Drain fillets on paper towels and keep them warm.

To make white wine sauce: melt butter in a saucepan, stir in flour off the heat and pour in the reserved fish stock.

Bring to a boil, stirring constantly, and simmer for 2 minutes. Add the light cream and bring back to a boil. Adjust seasoning and simmer sauce for 2–3 minutes or until it is of a coating consistency; keep the sauce warm.

Cook mushrooms quickly in a pan with 1 tablespoon water and the lemon juice for 1–2 minutes or until tender.

Arrange fish fillets in a heatproof serving dish, coat them with the white wine sauce, sprinkle mushrooms on top and put a spoonful of Hollandaise sauce on each

fillet. Cook under a heated broiler for 1–2 minutes or until glazed (lightly browned) and serve immediately with 'fish' potatoes.

'Fish' Potatoes
Peel 3 medium potatoes and quarter them lengthwise. Pare away sharp edges with a peeler and shape into ovals. Cook in a pan of boiling salted water for about 7 minutes, drain and return to pan. Cover with foil and lid and cook 4–5 minutes longer over very low heat or until tender. This prevents potatoes from breaking and makes them dry and tender.

Sole bonne femme is glazed under the broiler after coating with white sauce, mushrooms and Hollandaise sauce

Dessert

Dacquoise

¾ cup unblanched whole
    almonds
4 egg whites
1 cup sugar
pinch of cream of tartar

For filling
¾ cup (¼ lb) dried apricots
strip of lemon rind
½ cup sugar
¾ cup water
juice of ½ lemon
1 cup heavy cream, whipped
    until it holds a soft shape
sugar (to taste) – optional

For decoration
2 tablespoons confectioners'
    sugar
½ cup heavy cream, stiffly
    whipped
1 square (1 oz) semisweet
    chocolate, grated

*2 baking sheets lined with
    silicone paper; pastry bag;
    star tube*

Method
Set the oven at very low
(275°F) and mark an 8 inch
circle on each lined baking
sheet.

To grind the almonds, first
blanch them in boiling water,
drain and squeeze off the
skins, pat dry with paper
towels and work almonds
through a rotary cheese grinder
or in a blender.

Watchpoint: it is important
to use freshly blanched and
ground almonds so they are
not dry in texture. If you use
ready-blanched almonds, pour
boiling water over them and
let them soak for about 10
minutes before draining and
grinding.

Beat egg whites until they
hold a stiff peak, add 1 tablespoon of the sugar and the
cream of tartar and continue
beating 1 minute or until this
meringue mixture is glossy.
Fold in remaining sugar and
the ground almonds.

Divide mixture between 2
baking sheets, spreading it
carefully into the marked
circles. Bake 1 hour in the
heated oven. To test if the
meringues are done, lift a
corner of the paper and if it
peels away cleanly from the
bottom of the circle, the
meringues are baked. If not,
bake 15 minutes longer and
try again. Set aside to cool.

For filling: soak apricots if
necessary, according to the
package directions. Simmer
them gently in their soaking
liquid or in water to cover
with the strip of lemon rind.
When tender, remove lemon
rind and work apricots through
a sieve or purée in a blender,
and let them stand until cool.
Heat sugar with water until
dissolved, add lemon juice and
boil for 3 minutes to make a
lemon syrup. Stir one-quarter
to one-third of the apricot
purée into the whipped cream
and add sugar to taste, if you
like. Sandwich the meringue
layers together with this filling.

Sprinkle the top with confectioners' sugar; fill stiffly
whipped cream into the pastry
bag, fitted with a star tube,
and decorate the edge with
rosettes of cream; top these
with grated chocolate.

Dilute remaining apricot
purée with lemon syrup and
serve this sauce separately.

*To test if the meringues are cooked, lift a corner of the paper; it
should peel away easily*

*Spread one meringue round with apricot-flavored cream and
sandwich the layers together*

Dacquoise is decorated with whipped cream and grated chocolate and served with apricot sauce

CHAFING DISH COOKING

Cooking in a chafing dish is one of the nicest ways to entertain. The hostess avoids last-minute work in the kitchen, the food is freshly cooked and at its best and guests have the added pleasure of seeing a dish prepared.

However, like any performance, chafing dish cooking must be carefully planned in advance. All the ingredients must be ready at hand, measured and prepared when necessary, before you begin cooking.

In a good chafing dish, the burner under the pan is easily adjustable with a high setting for flaming and a low setting for keeping food warm. If you are unfamiliar with the burner and pan or with chafing dish cooking in general, start with simple dishes, such as smothered salmon or deviled sardines and avoid recipes like beef Stroganoff that depend on split-second timing.

Kinds of Chafing Dishes

There are several types available. Basically, chafing dishes are large, shallow frying pans that are fitted with some kind of burner. The most popular combination is a pan made of stainless steel with a copper base set on a small frame with a sterno or gas burner. More expensive models have a solid copper pan with a tin lining so the heat is distributed evenly and the contents of the pan are less likely to burn.

In old-fashioned chafing dishes, the pan is set over a shallow water bath with the burner underneath. The pan, often made of silver or silver plate, never gets very hot and although it is impossible to flame dishes, it is ideal for keeping food warm. Electric chafing dishes are also available.

A less elegant, but efficient substitute for a chafing dish is an electric frying pan. The heat is easy to control with very high and very low settings.

Any shallow frying pan, preferably with a heavy base, can be used as a chafing dish if it is placed over a portable burner. The burner must be adjustable with a high heat for flaming; candle-type warmers are inadequate.

The **lobster Newburg** and **deviled lobster** recipes in Volume 10 can be made easily in a chafing dish.

To 'Flamber' Dishes

Dishes are flamed (flambéed) with a liquor such as brandy or a fortified wine like sherry. Heat the liquor or wine until it is almost boiling so that it catches fire easily, then pour it, flaming, over the dish. The food must be hot and sizzling, otherwise the flame will go out. Alternatively, the liquor may be heated with the food, then flamed.

Flaming should slightly singe surface of food; alcohol is burned out of liquor so that the juices that remain give color and flavor to food and sauce. Flaming also burns up excess fat.

FISH

Spanish Lobster

1½ lb cooked lobster meat
¼ cup olive oil
3 onions, finely sliced
3 tomatoes, peeled, seeded and cut in strips
salt and pepper
6 tablespoons sherry (optional)
¾ cup fish or chicken stock
squeeze of lemon juice
1 tablespoon chopped chives

Method
Heat the oil in the chafing dish, add the onion and cook gently until transparent and just beginning to brown. Add the tomatoes, season and cook 5–6 minutes until pulpy. Put in the lobster meat, pour over the sherry, if using, bring to a boil and flame.

Add the stock, lower the heat and cook the mixture gently for 2–3 minutes until the lobster is very hot — there should be just enough sauce to coat the lobster. Add the lemon juice, taste for seasoning and sprinkle with chives. Serve with boiled rice or buttered toast.

Deviled Sardines

3 cans (3¾ oz each) sardines in oil
½ cup boiling water
1 tablespoon butter
salt and pepper
grated rind of ½ lemon and juice of 1 lemon
2 tablespoons tomato ketchup
1 tablespoon Worcestershire sauce
pinch of dry mustard
1 tablespoon chopped parsley
1 teaspoon mixed herbs (thyme, oregano)
8 slices of white bread, crusts removed, cut in rounds, toasted and buttered (for croûtes)

This is an easy dish for a quick snack; you will probably already have the ingredients in the kitchen cabinet.

Method
Drain the sardines thoroughly of oil and set them on a plate. Pour over ½ cup boiling water to wash off any remaining oil and tilt the plate to drain well.

Melt the butter in the chafing dish, add the sardines, season well and add the remaining ingredients except the croûtes. Heat gently until bubbling.

Have the croûtes ready on 4 individual hot serving plates. Lift the sardines onto them with a wide metal spatula and serve at once.

Smothered Salmon

3 cups flaked cooked fresh salmon or 2 cans (7¾ oz each) salmon
1 cup (¼ lb) mushrooms, chopped
1½ cups fresh white breadcrumbs
grated rind and juice of ½ lemon
1 tablespoon chopped parsley
1 teaspoon mixed herbs (tarragon, chives)
salt and pepper
5 tablespoons butter
2 teaspoons chopped parsley (for garnish)

This recipe can be used for any cooked flaked white fish.

Method

Mix the mushrooms, breadcrumbs, lemon rind and juice with the tablespoon of chopped parsley, herbs and seasoning. Melt 3 tablespoons butter in a chafing dish. Spread half mushroom mixture in chafing dish, scatter over the flaked salmon, cover with the rest of the mixture and dot with the remaining butter. Cover with buttered foil, add the lid and cook over a very low heat for 15–20 minutes or until the mixture starts to bubble. Sprinkle with the remaining parsley and serve from the chafing dish.

Creamed Shrimps

1½ lb cooked peeled shrimps
¼ cup butter
2 shallots, finely chopped
2 teaspoons curry powder
salt and pepper
2 tablespoons flour
2 cups milk or light cream
1 package frozen peas, thawed
4–6 slices of white bread, crusts removed, cut in triangles and toasted (for croûtes)

Method

Melt the butter in the chafing dish, add the shallot, curry powder and seasoning and cook gently for 2–3 minutes. Stir in the flour, add the milk or light cream and bring to a boil, stirring.

Add the peas and simmer 3–4 minutes. Add the shrimps, cover and heat gently for 5–8 minutes or until very hot. Taste for seasoning and spoon over croûtes in a hot serving dish.

MEAT

Sautéed Kidneys with Bacon

8 lambs' kidneys
8 slices of bacon
2 tablespoons melted butter (for brushing)
1 egg, beaten to mix
1 cup dry white breadcrumbs
3 tablespoons butter (for frying)
salt and pepper
1 tablespoon chopped parsley
juice of ½ lemon
8 slices of white bread, crusts removed, toasted and buttered (for croûtes)

4 skewers

Method

Skin the kidneys, if necessary, snip the cores with scissors and partly split them. Flatten them so they are 'butterflied' and thread 2 kidneys on each skewer. Brush them with melted butter, then with egg and roll them in breadcrumbs.

In a chafing dish melt 2 tablespoons of the butter for frying, put in the kidneys, cut side down, and sauté until brown; turn over and brown on the other side, allowing 3 minutes on each side for kidneys that are rare in the center. Take out and sprinkle with salt and pepper.

Wipe out chafing dish, fry the bacon until crisp and drain on paper towels. Discard the fat from the dish, wipe it out and melt the remaining butter. Put back the kidneys, sprinkle them with parsley and lemon juice and turn them until hot and coated with melted butter. Lay the bacon on top.

To serve, push the kidneys off the skewers onto the buttered toast by running the skewers between the prongs of a fork.

To cook the kidneys without egg and breadcrumb coating: cut the strips of bacon in half and roll them. Thread the rolls of bacon on the skewers with the kidneys and sauté in 1 tablespoon butter, allowing 2½ minutes on each side for rare kidneys. Transfer the kidneys to buttered toast and season. Melt 2 tablespoons more butter in the chafing dish, add the chopped parsley and the lemon juice, shake to mix well and pour over the kidneys.

Deviled Kidneys

Prepare and skewer kidneys as in sautéed kidneys and cook them for 2 minutes on each side. Take pan from the heat and spread each side of the kidneys with prepared hot or Dijon-style mustard. Continue cooking 1 minute on each side (for rare kidneys) and serve on buttered toast sprinkled with a squeeze of lemon juice.

Beef Stroganoff is an ideal meat recipe to prepare in a chafing dish

Beef Stroganoff

$1\frac{1}{2}$ lb beef fillet, cut in
   2 X $\frac{3}{8}$ X $\frac{3}{8}$ inch strips
$\frac{1}{4}$ cup butter
2 onions, sliced
2 cups ($\frac{1}{2}$ lb) mushrooms,
   sliced
$\frac{1}{4}$ cup brandy
salt and pepper
1 cup sour cream
1 cup rice, boiled (to serve)

Method
In the chafing dish melt half the butter and gently fry the onions until golden brown. Take out, add the mushrooms and cook until all the liquid has evaporated; add them to the onions. Wipe out the dish, melt the remaining butter and fry the steak over high heat in 2–3 batches, turning it so it browns on all sides.

Watchpoint: the steak must be fried quickly, a little at a time, so that it browns on the outside while the inside remains rare and the juices are not drawn out into the pan.

Put all the meat back into the pan, pour over the brandy and flame. Turn down the heat, season well, replace onions and mushrooms and cook gently 1–2 minutes until very hot. Stir in the sour cream, bring almost to a boil, taste for seasoning and serve with boiled rice.

POULTRY

Chicken with Mushrooms

6–8 cooked chicken pieces
5 tablespoons butter
$\frac{1}{4}$ teaspoon cayenne
$\frac{1}{2}$ teaspoon dry mustard
2 cups ($\frac{1}{2}$ lb) mushrooms
4 slices of white bread, crusts removed, cut in half and fried in 4 tablespoons oil and butter (for croûtes)
salt and pepper

Method
Cream 1 tablespoon of the butter with the cayenne and mustard. Score the chicken pieces and spread them well with the flavored butter, working it into the slits.

In a chafing dish heat 2 tablespoons more butter. Trim the mushroom stems level with the caps and fry the mushrooms gently in the butter until tender. Take them out and wipe out the pan.

Make the croûtes. Wipe out the pan again, melt the remaining 2 tablespoons butter and add the chicken, skin side down. Fry until golden-brown on all sides, starting over low heat and gradually increasing the heat. When the chicken is browned and very hot, return the mushrooms to the pan, add seasoning and heat, shaking the pan to prevent the chicken mixture from sticking, for 1–2 minutes. Serve on the croûtes.

EGGS

Eggs en Cocotte with Cheese

8 eggs
3 slices of Gruyère cheese, cut in 1 inch squares
salt and pepper
$\frac{1}{2}$ cup heavy cream
1 teaspoon paprika (for sprinkling)

8 cocottes or individual baking dishes

Any recipe for eggs en cocotte (baked eggs) can be cooked in a chafing dish.

Method
Half fill the chafing dish with boiling salted water. Generously butter the cocottes or baking dishes, put 2–3 squares of cheese in each and break 1 egg on top of each. Season, add 1 tablespoon cream and sprinkle with a pinch of paprika.

Stand the cocottes in the water so it comes just up to the rims of the dishes, cover the pan with a lid and cook very slowly, so the water is almost simmering, for 7–8 minutes or until the eggs are partly set.

Deviled Anchovy Eggs

8 eggs
$\frac{1}{4}$ cup butter
1 teaspoon prepared hot mustard
2 tablespoons tomato sauce
1 tablespoon Worcestershire sauce
salt and pepper
8 slices of white bread, cut in rounds, toasted and buttered (for croûtes)
1 tablespoon anchovy paste (or to taste) – for croûtes

Method
Soft-cook the eggs in gently simmering water, allowing 5 minutes from the time the water returns to a boil. Drain and cool in cold water for 7–8 minutes, then peel them carefully and keep in cold water until needed.

Make the croûtes, spread generously with anchovy paste and keep warm on 4 individual plates.

In a chafing dish melt the butter, then add the mustard, tomato and Worcestershire sauces and mix well. Drain the eggs, dry them on paper towels and add them to the deviled mixture when it is simmering. Break up the eggs coarsely with a potato masher or fork, season and cook the mixture over low heat, stirring, until very hot and starting to set. Taste for seasoning and spoon at once onto the croûtes and serve.

For pineapple flambé 1, cook slices of pineapple in butter and sugar, flame with brandy and serve them on slices of cake

DESSERTS

Pineapple Flambé 1

1 pineapple, peeled, cored and
   cut in slices
sugar (for sprinkling)
6–8 tablespoons butter
4–6 slices of dry sponge or
   angel food cake
¼ cup brandy or rum

Method
Sprinkle the pineapple with sugar and reserve. In a chafing dish heat half the butter and brown the slices of cake on both sides over gentle heat, sprinkling the cake lightly with sugar during frying. Arrange the cake on a hot platter.

Wipe out the dish, melt the remaining butter, add the pineapple slices, sprinkle them well with sugar, turn over and cook quickly until just beginning to brown. Sprinkle with sugar, turn over and brown on the other side. Pour in the brandy or rum, turn the heat up to full, flame and arrange the pineapple on the cake while still flaming. Pour over any juice and serve at once.

Other Flambéed Fruits

Fresh fruits are best flambéed according to the recipe for pineapple flambé 1 — any distilled liquor like brandy, rum or kirsch may be used.

For drained canned fruits and for juicy fresh fruits like strawberries, follow recipe for pineapple flambé 2.

Pineapple Flambé 2

1 pineapple, peeled, cored and
   cut in slices
2–3 tablespoons sugar
3–4 tablespoons kirsch
3–4 tablespoons brandy

Method
Sprinkle the pineapple lightly with sugar, lay it in a chafing dish and sprinkle with a little kirsch. Set over moderate heat and heat until hot, shaking dish to prevent pineapple from sticking, then sprinkle with the remaining kirsch. When hot, scatter pineapple with more sugar and sprinkle over the brandy. Shake the dish well, tipping it so it flames. Serve while still flaming.

Peaches or Bananas with Liqueur

Peaches and bananas are a good choice for chafing dish cooking as they cook quickly. This recipe can also be used for drained canned fruits like figs, pears and apricots.

Scale, peel, halve and pit the peaches or peel and thickly slice bananas. Melt 1–2 tablespoons butter in a chafing dish, add the fruit, sprinkle with 1–2 tablespoons sugar and fry gently on both sides until the fruit is lightly browned with caramelized sugar. Add about ¼ cup brandy, rum or orange liqueur such as Grand Marnier, Curaçao or Triple Sec and serve at once.

To peel and cut fresh pineapple, slice off bottom of pineapple with serrated-edged knife. Hold pineapple firmly and with a sharp stainless steel knife cut down between the "eyes" at a 45° angle. The pineapple eyes should come out easily in strips. Remove plume, slice flesh thinly and cut out core with a grapefruit corer. This method of peeling and coring disposes of eyes but avoids waste.

For Pineapple Flambe 1: slices of sponge cake are browned in butter in the chafing dish.

Cherries Jubilee

1 can (1 lb) pitted Bing
   cherries
1 teaspoon arrowroot mixed
   to a paste with 1 tablespoon
   water
¼ cup kirsch or brandy
1 pint vanilla ice cream

Serves 3 people.

Method
Drain the cherries and reserve them. In a chafing dish heat the cherry juice until it boils and stir in the arrowroot paste until the sauce thickens. Add the reserved cherries and heat gently until they are very hot. Take from the heat.

In a separate small pan or large ladle, heat the kirsch or brandy. Replace the chafing dish with the cherry mixture on the heat, flame the kirsch or brandy and add to the cherries. To serve, spoon the mixture, while still flaming, over scoops of vanilla ice cream in individual dishes.

Roast suckling pig, with a savory stuffing and accompanied by baked apples with apricot, makes a spectacular party dish (recipe is on page 62)

FESTIVE PARTY DISHES

When planning dinners for a special occasion there are plenty of exciting alternatives to turkey. Order a suckling pig from your butcher and stuff it with a spicy rice and pistachio filling; or invest in a rich goose and braise it with red wine or spice it with mustard and paprika.

If you enjoy experimenting, try making Yorkshire pie – a goose stuffed with a pheasant (that has been stuffed with a tongue) and covered with flaky pastry. In medieval times, these dishes would have been offered simultaneously as part of a lavish banquet, but today, with our more modest appetites, just one of them makes the foundation for a fabulous feast.

Roast Suckling Pig

Fresh suckling pigs are not easy to find unless you live in a hog-raising area or in a large city, but most butchers and some specialty markets will supply frozen ones. Sizes of pigs range from 12 lb–25 lb. The smaller the pig, the more delicate the meat. For large pigs, over 18 lb, allow 1 lb per person; smaller pigs serve fewer people so a 12 lb pig is enough for 10.

If your oven is large enough to accommodate it, stretch the pig's forelegs straight forward from the body and the hind legs out backwards. Alternatively, the legs may be tucked under the body, so the animal occupies less space.

Set the oven at very hot (450°F).

Clean and wipe the pig thoroughly and fill it with the chosen stuffing; pack it in well so the pig looks plump and sew it up with a trussing needle and string. A 12 lb pig needs about 10 cups stuffing and a 25 lb pig takes 18–20 cups stuffing.

Set the pig in a roasting pan and brush it with 1–2 tablespoons oil. Use a wooden block to prop open the mouth and roast in heated oven, allowing 30 minutes per lb. A meat thermometer inserted in the ham (rump) should register 170°F. After 15 minutes cooking turn oven to moderately low (325°F) and baste every 15 minutes. Halfway through roasting sprinkle pig with flour to help crisp the skin — this crackling is often regarded as the best part of the animal.

Arrange roasted pig on a bed of rosemary or bay tree branches on a large platter and place a lemon in the mouth; alternatively decorate the dish with fresh fruit and place an apple in the mouth.

To carve a pig: cut along backbone from head to tail. Cut around the head, then ease away skin from one side in one piece. If the layer of fat underneath is very thick, trim some away and discard it. Cut around the ham down to the bone, then carve ham in diagonal slices like the breast of a chicken. Cut along one side of the backbone and down close to the ribs to loosen the meat; cut it in slices. Finally, carve the shoulder meat in slanting slices. Carve the other side in the same way. Serve each person a portion of the crisp skin with the meat.

If you prefer not to display the whole suckling pig at the table, carve meat from the carcass as described and arrange it on a platter.

When serving hot: try stuffing the pig with onion stuffing and serve it with cranberry sauce, pan gravy and baked apples with apricot; alternatively stuff it with rice and pistachio stuffing and serve it with unthickened gravy made with white wine and a spoonful of red currant jelly.

When serving cold; stuff the pig with onion stuffing and serve it with chilled tart apple sauce. Alternatively pierce the skin of the pig in several places with a sharp knife before cooking and rub pig inside and out with a mixture of 2 teaspoons salt, 1 teaspoon ground cinnamon, 1 teaspoon ground ginger, 1 teaspoon ground allspice, ½ teaspoon ground nutmeg and ½ teaspoon ground cloves. Fill it with chestnut stuffing (see Volume 8) and roast as above. During the last half hour of roasting baste the pig with honey to give a shiny glaze to the skin.

Accompaniments for Suckling Pig

Baked Apples with Apricot

6–8 medium-sized tart apples
3 tablespoons apricot jam
¼ cup dark brown sugar
grated rind and juice of 1 large lemon
3 tablespoons butter

Method
Set oven at moderately hot (375°F).

Wipe the apples, core and pare about ½ inch of the peel from the top of each. Mix together sugar, lemon rind and juice and butter and pack into the apple cavities. Set in a baking dish, pour in just enough hot water to cover the bottom and bake in heated oven for 25–30 minutes or until the apples are tender.

Cool slightly, then carefully scoop out about 1 tablespoon of the soft apple pulp, taking care not to break or spoil the shape of skins. Mix pulp with apricot jam and add extra sugar and lemon juice to taste if needed. Fill apples with this mixture and reheat to serve.

Fill apples with butter and lemon mixture, then bake

Onion Stuffing

3 medium onions, finely chopped
1 cup butter
liver and kidneys of the pig, ducts removed and finely chopped
8 cups fresh white breadcrumbs
3 tablespoons sage or marjoram
¼ cup chopped parsley
salt and pepper
3 eggs, beaten to mix

Makes about 10 cups.

Method
Cook onion in butter until soft. Add the liver and kidneys and sauté briskly for 2–3 minutes or until brown. Cool, mix with the breadcrumbs, herbs and plenty of seasoning and stir in the beaten eggs.

Rice and Pistachio Stuffing

2½ cups rice
1 cup shelled pistachios
6 tablespoons butter
2 onions, finely chopped
5–6 cups chicken stock
1 cup raisins
½ teaspoon ground cinnamon
½ teaspoon ground allspice
¼ teaspoon ground nutmeg
salt and pepper

Makes about 10 cups.

Method
In a flameproof casserole melt the butter and cook onion until soft. Stir in the rice and cook 2–3 minutes until the grains are transparent. Add 5 cups stock with the raisins, spices and seasoning, cover and bring to a boil.

Bake in a moderately hot

oven (375°F) for 15 minutes, add more stock if the pan is dry and continue baking 5–7 minutes or until rice is tender. Cool mixture, add the pistachios and taste for seasoning before stuffing into pig.

Baked Stuffed Ham

9–10 lb completely cooked ham, on the bone
2 egg yolks, beaten to mix
½ cup browned breadcrumbs
2 tablespoons oil

For stuffing
1 medium onion, chopped
¼ cup butter
3 cups fresh white breadcrumbs
2 teaspoons mixed herbs (thyme, tarragon, marjoram)
3 tablespoons chopped parsley
salt and pepper

Serves 10–12 people.

Method
Cut ham in slices down to the bone but do not detach. Set oven at moderate (350°F).

To make stuffing: cook onion in butter until soft, mix with breadcrumbs and herbs and season well. Sandwich this stuffing between slices of ham and reshape the ham, fastening with skewers if necessary. Brush well with egg yolks and sprinkle with browned breadcrumbs. Heat the oil in a roasting pan, put in the ham and bake in heated oven, basting occasionally, for 30–40 minutes until crumbs are brown and crisp and the ham is very hot. Serve hot with sweet potatoes, succotash or braised chestnuts.

Succotash

2 cups fresh shelled baby lima beans
2 cups corn kernels
2 tablespoons butter
1 teaspoon sugar
¼ cup water
salt and pepper
½ cup heavy cream

There are many short cuts to succotash, but none compares to that made with fresh corn and baby lima beans.

Method
Cook the beans in boiling salted water for 15–18 minutes or until tender. Drain, refresh under cold running water and combine in a saucepan with the corn, butter, sugar, water, and salt and pepper to taste.

Cook mixture over a low heat for 10–15 minutes and drain. Add the cream and heat thoroughly without boiling.

Duchesse Potatoes
Mash 6–8 medium-sized boiled potatoes with 1 cup milk, ¼ cup butter and seasoning. Beat in 3 egg yolks.

Chapon Demi-deuil (Capon in Half-mourning)

5–6 lb capon
small can whole truffles
bunch of watercress (for garnish)
Duchesse potatoes (for serving)

For stuffing
1 lb (2 cups) lean veal, ground
2 egg whites
salt
pepper
1 cup heavy cream
small can truffle pieces

For poaching
1 onion, quartered
1 carrot, quartered
1 stalk of celery, cut in pieces
6 peppercorns
bouquet garni
water

For velouté sauce
3 tablespoons butter
2 tablespoons flour
2 cups well-flavored chicken stock
squeeze of lemon juice
3 egg yolks
1 cup heavy cream

Trussing needle and string or poultry pins

Serves 6 people.

Method
Thickly slice the whole truffles, and with your fingers insert the slices (reserving a few) under skin of capon along the breast, lifting the skin gently from the meat so it does not break. Chop leftover slices of truffle and reserve their liquid.

To make stuffing: pound the veal in a mortar and pestle. Beat egg whites until frothy and gradually work into the veal. Alternatively the veal may be worked with the egg whites in a blender for a few seconds until smooth. Add salt and pepper and gradually work in the cream, placing the bowl over a pan of ice water if the mixture seems very soft. Season well.

Watchpoint: thorough working is essential when making this stuffing, otherwise it may separate.

Drain the truffle pieces, reserving the liquid, and add them to the leftover chopped slices. Stir half of this truffle mixture into the stuffing. Spoon stuffing into the capon and truss or fasten with poultry pins.

Place capon in a kettle with the ingredients for poaching, add water to cover and the lid and simmer 2 hours or until bird is very tender.

To make velouté sauce: melt butter in a saucepan, stir in flour off the heat and pour in stock. Bring to a boil, stirring, and simmer 2 minutes. Add lemon juice and taste for seasoning.

Take capon from the heat, remove trussing strings or poultry pins, cool slightly, then drain and keep warm.

Add liaison to sauce: mix egg yolks with cream, stir in a little hot sauce, add this mixture to the remaining sauce and heat, stirring, until it thickens slightly. Add the remaining truffle mixture and all the truffle liquid and taste for seasoning. Arrange capon on a platter, spoon over a little sauce and serve the rest separately. Garnish the dish with watercress and serve Duchesse potatoes separately.

BONING A BIRD

1 With a sharp knife, slit skin down back of bird. Work the skin and flesh away from the carcass with a knife until the leg joint is reached; sever it.

2 Holding the knob of the leg joint in one hand, cut away the flesh and scrape thigh bone clean.

3 Continue cleaning drumstick until the whole leg bone is free of flesh. Remove this bone from carcass and repeat the same process on other side of bird.

4 Next sever one wing joint

from carcass, and discard. Separate white meat from breastbone. Free second wing joint and remaining breast meat in the same way.

5 Cut the skin away from the top of the breastbone very carefully. Be sure not to split the skin but keep both sides of the bird joined.

6 Lay the bird, skin side down, flat on a board ready to stuff it.

Note: where recipes specify to bone, leaving in leg and wing joints, do not remove these as directed above.

1

2

3

4

5

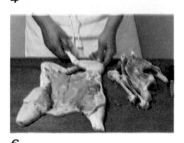

6

Christmas Stuffed Goose

6–7 lb plump goose
2½–3 lb roasting chicken
1 squab
2 tablespoons butter
1 teaspoon salt
½ teaspoon allspice
flour (for sprinkling)
2 tablespoons melted butter
little stock (made from bones of the birds), or water
baked apples with apricot (for garnish – see page 62)

For stuffing
1½ lb loose sausage meat
1 cup (½ lb) cooked ham, ground
livers of the birds, ground
3 shallots, finely chopped
2 cups (½ lb) mushrooms, chopped
1½ cups fresh white breadcrumbs
1 teaspoon sage
¼ teaspoon allspice
black pepper, freshly ground
1–2 eggs, beaten to mix

For gravy
2 teaspoons flour
1½ cups well-flavored stock (made from bones of the birds)
juice of ½ lemon
dash of Tabasco

Trussing needle and string or poultry pins

Serves 10 people.

Method
Bone the birds (see left).

Set oven at hot (400°F).

Lay birds flat. Cream 2 tablespoons butter with salt and allspice and spread over birds.

To make stuffing: mix all ingredients except egg together and season well. Stir in enough egg to bind and spread over cut surfaces of birds. Lay chicken, skin side down, on top of cut side of

goose, then put squab on chicken in the same way. Roll the goose around the two birds and sew up securely.

Shape into a roll and tie at 2 inch intervals with string. Set in a roasting pan, sprinkle generously with flour and baste well with melted butter. Roast in heated oven, basting often with the fat that runs from the goose, for 30 minutes or until goose is brown. Turn down oven to moderately hot (375°F) and continue roasting for 1–1¼ hours longer or until a meat thermometer inserted in the center registers 170°F.

Watchpoint: if the juices in the pan show signs of burning, add a little stock or water.

Transfer goose to a platter, remove trussing strings or poultry pins and keep warm.

To prepare gravy: discard as much fat as possible from the pan, stir in flour and brown. Pour in stock, add lemon juice and Tabasco and bring to a boil, stirring to dissolve pan juices. Taste for seasoning; strain.

Garnish the stuffed goose with baked apples with apricot and spoon over a little gravy, serving the rest separately. Braised celery, braised onions and small roast potatoes are good accompaniments.

Braised Goose

8–9 lb goose
$2\frac{1}{2}$–3 cups brown sauce
2 teaspoons arrowroot (mixed to a paste with 2 tablespoons water) – optional

For stuffing
2 medium onions, finely chopped
3 tablespoons butter
$1\frac{1}{2}$ lb ground pork or loose sausage meat
$1\frac{1}{2}$ cups fresh white breadcrumbs
2 tablespoons chopped parsley
1 tablespoon mixed herbs (sage, marjoram, thyme)
$\frac{1}{4}$ teaspoon ground mace
salt and pepper
2 small eggs, beaten to mix

For braising
3 tablespoons butter or oil
3 onions, diced
3 carrots, diced
2 medium turnips, diced
3–4 stalks of celery, diced
large bouquet garni
8 peppercorns
$2\frac{1}{2}$–3 cups well-flavored stock
1 cup red wine

For braised chestnuts
$1\frac{1}{2}$ lb chestnuts
1 tablespoon oil
1 onion, finely sliced
2 cups well-flavored stock

Trussing needle and string or poultry pins

Serves 6–8 people.

Method
Set oven at moderate (350°F).

To make stuffing: cook onion in butter until soft, add the pork or sausage meat and cook, stirring, until it is browned. Pour off excess fat, let cool and stir in the breadcrumbs, herbs, mace and plenty of seasoning and bind with beaten egg. Stuff goose and truss it with string or fasten with poultry pins.

To braise: in a large flameproof casserole heat butter or oil, add vegetables, cover and cook over low heat for 5–7 minutes or until soft. Put goose on top, add bouquet garni and peppercorns at the side and pour in $2\frac{1}{2}$ cups stock. Raise heat and reduce liquid by about one-quarter, then add the wine. Cover casserole with foil, then with the lid and braise in heated oven for $2\frac{1}{2}$–3 hours or until bird is very tender, basting often. After about 2 hours, remove the lid and foil and continue to braise, basting well so the skin is crisp and adding a little more stock, if necessary.

To braise chestnuts: skin the nuts, soften onion in oil in a flameproof casserole, spread chestnuts on top, pour over stock, add seasoning, cover and reserve. Forty-five minutes before goose is cooked, put chestnuts in oven and braise until nuts are tender. Remove lid and boil to reduce all liquid until chestnuts are glazed and shiny.

Take out goose, remove trussing strings or poultry pins, set it on a large platter and keep warm. Strain cooking liquid and skim well to remove fat. Add liquid to the brown sauce and simmer 5–6 minutes until reduced and well flavored. If necessary, stir in arrowroot paste to thicken sauce slightly and bring just to a boil. Taste for seasoning, pour a little sauce over the goose and serve the rest separately. Surround goose with the garnish of the braised chestnuts and serve with château potatoes.

To Skin Chestnuts
Pierce each nut with a pointed knife. In a saucepan cover the chestnuts with cold water, bring to a boil and take from the heat. Lift nuts from the water with a slotted spoon, a few at a time, hold them with a cloth and strip away the shell and inner skin with a small sharp knife. If the skin does not peel easily, put the nuts back in the hot water for another minute.

If the water cools, bring it just back to a boil; do not allow the water to boil for more than $\frac{1}{2}$ minute or the nuts will overcook and the peel and skin will be impossible to remove.

Brown Sauce

2 tablespoons finely diced carrot
2 tablespoons finely diced onion
1 tablespoon finely diced celery
2–3 tablespoons oil
$1\frac{1}{2}$ tablespoons flour
$1\frac{1}{2}$ teaspoons tomato paste
$2\frac{1}{2}$ cups stock
$1\frac{1}{2}$ cups red wine

Makes $2\frac{1}{2}$–3 cups.

Method
In a heavy saucepan cook vegetables in oil over medium heat until they begin to brown. Stir in flour and cook until a rich brown. Take from heat, stir in tomato paste and stock and bring to a boil. Simmer about 30 minutes with pan half-covered. Add wine and cook, uncovered, for 20 minutes. Strain and use as required.

Spiced Goose

8–9 lb goose
$\frac{1}{4}$ cup oil
1$\frac{1}{2}$ tablespoons prepared
    mustard
2 tablespoons chili sauce
1 teaspoon anchovy paste
2 cloves of garlic, crushed

For stuffing
3 lb ground pork or beef
$\frac{3}{4}$ lb piece of bacon,
    ground
liver of the goose, ground
1 tablespoon mixed herbs
    (thyme, marjoram, savory)
few drops of Tabasco
1$\frac{1}{2}$ teaspoons paprika
1$\frac{1}{2}$ teaspoons anchovy paste
1 cup fresh white breadcrumbs
salt
black pepper, freshly ground
4–5 tablespoons sherry, or
    1 large egg (beaten to mix)

For braising
1$\frac{1}{2}$ cups well-flavored stock
    (made from the goose bones)
    or veal stock
2 onions, sliced
2 carrots, sliced
bouquet garni

For gravy
2 cups well-flavored stock
    (made from the goose bones)
1 tablespoon ketchup
1 tablespoon apricot jam
kneaded butter (made with
    2 tablespoons butter,
    1 tablespoon flour)
1 large dill pickle, cut in strips

For garnish
24–30 small onions, blanched
    and peeled
18–24 small carrots, peeled
3 tablespoons butter
1$\frac{1}{2}$ tablespoons sugar
chopped mint, for sprinkling
château potatoes (see right)

Trussing needle and string or
*   poultry pins*

Serves 8 people.

Method
Bone the goose, leaving in leg and wing bones, and lay it flat on a board. Use bones to make at least 3$\frac{1}{2}$ cups well-flavored stock for gravy and for braising. Mix together 2 tablespoons oil, mustard, chili sauce and anchovy paste and add the crushed garlic. Spread this on the cut surface of the goose.

To make stuffing: mix all ingredients together, season well and moisten with sherry or beaten egg. Spread stuffing on the goose, sew it up and reshape the bird. Truss neatly or fasten with poultry pins.

Set oven at moderate (350°F).

Brush surface of goose with remaining oil, then brown it on all sides over low heat in a large flameproof casserole. Set goose on its back and pour around 1$\frac{1}{2}$ cups stock. Add onion, carrot and bouquet garni, bring to a boil, cover and braise in heated oven 2$\frac{1}{2}$–3 hours or until a meat thermometer inserted in center of bird registers 170°F.

To make garnish: in a pan put the onions with 2 tablespoons butter and sprinkle with 1 tablespoon sugar. Cover and cook gently for about 10 minutes, shaking pan occasionally, or until onions are tender and caramelized. Put carrots in a pan with water to cover and add remaining sugar, 1 tablespoon butter and a pinch of salt. Cover, simmer 10–15 minutes or until tender, then remove lid and boil until all water has evaporated and carrots are shiny. Sprinkle with mint just before serving.

Cook château potatoes for garnish.

To make gravy: mix stock, ketchup and apricot jam together, bring to a boil and strain. Reheat, thicken by whisking in kneaded butter, add pickle and taste for seasoning.

Note: if made from the cooking juices, this gravy would be too fatty.

Lift out goose, remove trussing strings or poultry pins and brown it well below a heated broiler until skin is crisp. Arrange on a platter, surround with vegetable garnish and heat a few moments in a low oven if necessary. Reheat the gravy and serve separately.

Château Potatoes
Peel 12–16 small potatoes, cut in quarters lengthwise, and trim off sharp edges with a vegetable peeler. Blanch in cold water, bring to a boil and drain. If using new potatoes, scrub them with a small brush.

In a flameproof casserole melt 4–5 tablespoons butter, add potatoes and cook over moderate heat until golden brown all over, occasionally shaking to turn them and prevent them from sticking. Sprinkle them lightly with salt, cover and bake in a hot oven (400°F) for 10–12 minutes or until the potatoes are tender.

Note: photographs and instructions for boning a bird are given on page 64.

Yorkshire Pie

6–7 lb plump goose
2$\frac{1}{2}$–3 lb pheasant or chicken
$\frac{3}{4}$–1 lb whole calf's tongue
3 cup quantity flaky pastry
    (made with 3 cups flour,
    $\frac{1}{2}$ teaspoon salt,
    9 tablespoons butter,
    9 tablespoons shortening,
    $\frac{3}{4}$–1 cup ice water)
1 onion
1 carrot
6 peppercorns
salt
1–2 bay leaves
black pepper, freshly ground
2 tablespoons butter
2 cups well-flavored stock
    (made from the goose and
    pheasant or chicken bones,
    1 onion, 1 carrot, stalk of
    celery, bouquet garni)
1 envelope gelatin (optional)
1 egg, beaten with $\frac{1}{2}$ teaspoon
    salt (for glaze)

For stuffing
1 small onion, finely chopped
1$\frac{1}{2}$ tablespoons butter
1$\frac{1}{2}$ lb ground pork
1$\frac{1}{2}$ cups fresh white
    breadcrumbs
2 teaspoons mixed herbs
    (thyme, oregano, marjoram,
    sage)
1 tablespoon chopped parsley
pinch of ground mace or
    allspice
1 egg, beaten to mix

Deep 12–14 inch rectangular
*   or oval baking dish*

Serves 8–10 people.

Method
Simmer tongue with onion, carrot, peppercorns, little salt and bay leaves to flavor in water to cover for 1$\frac{1}{2}$ hours or until very tender. Cool to lukewarm in the liquid, drain, plunge it in a bowl of cold water to make it easy to handle, peel off the skin and remove small bones at the

root of the tongue.

Bone the birds, removing leg and wing bones and taking care not to break the skin. Reserve bones for stock. Season the cut surface of the birds, then place the tongue inside the pheasant or chicken and put that inside the goose. Roll up the goose, rub the surface with butter and sprinkle with seasoning.

To make stuffing: cook onion in butter until soft and mix with the pork, breadcrumbs and herbs. Add mace or allspice, season well and bind with beaten egg. Line bottom and sides of baking dish with three-quarters of the stuffing, keeping the rest for the top. Put goose in the center and cover with remaining stuffing in a thin layer.

Make stock from the bones. Strain it and cool — it should be jellied. If stock is not jellied, sprinkle over gelatin, let stand 5 minutes and heat gently until gelatin is dissolved before adding stock to the pie.

Set oven at hot (400°F).

Roll out the pastry 1 inch larger than the baking dish and cover the top of the pie, making a small hole in the center to allow steam to escape and for pouring in stock when pie is cooked. Trim edge and decorate top with leaves and flowers made from the trimmings. Brush with egg glaze and bake in center of heated oven for 30—40 minutes or until pastry is browned. Cover pie with foil, tucking it down around the edge, turn down the oven to moderate (350°F) and continue baking for 1½—2 hours or until a skewer inserted in the center for 1 minute is very hot when withdrawn. Cool.

Warm stock and pour enough into the pie to fill it. Chill before serving.

Place cooked tongue inside boned pheasant (or chicken)

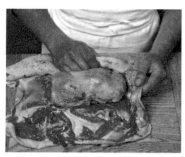

Put pheasant inside the boned goose and roll up neatly

Lay the stuffed goose in the stuffing-lined baking dish

Yorkshire pie—a tongue is stuffed inside a pheasant or chicken that is stuffed inside a goose

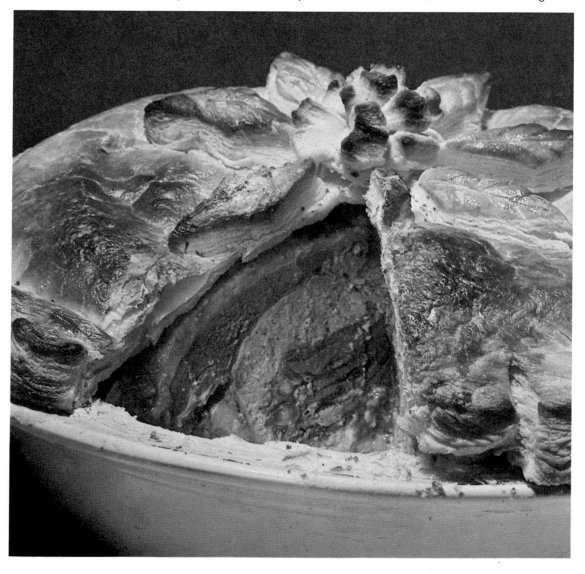

An array of festive cookies are: (in front) sugar-coated German pfeffernüsse surrounded by fruit-topped Polish mazurki, (behind at left and 'birds' on tree) American sugar cookies, and (behind at right) Dutch speculaas decorated with halved almonds

PARTY DESSERTS AND COOKIES

Whether it's the end to an elegant dinner or an accompaniment for coffee when friends stop by, these special desserts and cookies will be wonderful surprises.

Make the cookies ahead of time and arrange them on an attractive platter for a festive center-piece or, at Christmas, hang them from colorful strings on the tree.

Pfeffernüsse
(German 'Peppery Nuts')

1 cup sugar
2 eggs, separated
2 cups flour
1½ teaspoons ground cinnamon
¼ teaspoon ground ginger
¼ teaspoon ground cardamom
¼ teaspoon ground allspice
¼ teaspoon ground white
   pepper
3 tablespoons finely chopped
   candied citron
grated rind of 1 lemon
2–3 tablespoons whole
   almonds, blanched and
   ground

To finish
3–4 tablespoons rum
confectioners' sugar
   (for rolling)
candied cherries, cut in pieces

Makes 33–36 pfeffernüsse.

Method
Beat half the sugar with egg yolks until mixture is light and fluffy. Sift flour with all the spices and stir into egg yolk mixture. Whip egg whites until they hold a stiff peak and beat in remaining sugar until glossy. Stir gently into flour mixture with citron, lemon rind and almonds. Cover bowl and let stand in refrigerator overnight.

Set oven at moderately hot (375°F) and butter a baking sheet. Roll and press the rather crumbly mixture into walnut-sized balls, set on baking sheet and bake in heated oven 18–20 minutes or until lightly browned. Sprinkle them with rum while warm and roll in confectioners' sugar.

Store in an airtight container for at least a week to mellow — pfeffernüsse will keep well for several weeks.

Just before serving, roll again in confectioners' sugar and top with a piece of candied cherry.

Mazurki Bakaliowe
(Polish Fruit and Nut Cookies)

2 cups flour
¼ teaspoon salt
½ cup butter
1 cup sugar
1 egg
3 tablespoons light cream

For topping
1¼ cups raisins
1¼ cups chopped dates
1½ cups chopped figs
1 cup chopped almonds or
   walnuts
½ cup sugar
2 eggs
juice of 1 lemon
juice of 1 orange
½ cup candied cherries, cut in
   pieces
½ cup chopped candied orange
   peel

15 X 11 inch jelly roll pan

These are traditional Easter cookies. Makes about 80 cookies.

Method
Set oven at moderate (350°F) and grease jelly roll pan.

To make dough: sift flour and salt into a bowl and work in butter with the fingertips until mixture resembles crumbs. Stir in sugar. Mix egg with cream and stir into the flour to form a smooth dough. Pat out in the jelly roll pan and bake in heated oven 20 minutes or until browned.

To make topping: mix raisins, dates, figs, nuts, sugar, eggs and fruit juices very thoroughly together and spread on the dough. Continue baking 15–20 minutes, cool and scatter over the cherries and orange peel. Before quite cold, cut in 1 X 2 inch rectangles.

Store in an airtight container.

Ciastka Miodowe
(Polish Honey Cookies)

½ cup honey
½ cup sugar
1 egg
1 egg yolk
2 cups flour
½ teaspoon baking soda
¼ teaspoon ground cinnamon
¼ teaspoon ground nutmeg
¼ teaspoon ground cloves
¼ teaspoon ground ginger
1 egg, beaten with ¼ teaspoon
   salt (for glaze)

For filling
6 squares (6 oz) semisweet
   chocolate, chopped
½ cup heavy cream
1 teaspoon vanilla
1¼ cups confectioners' sugar
1 cup whole almonds, browned
   and ground

Makes about 18 cookies.

Method
To make dough: warm honey, stir into sugar and add egg and egg yolk. Beat until thick and light. Sift flour with soda and spices and stir into mixture to form a firm dough. Cover and let stand 1 hour or overnight.

Set oven at moderate (350°F). Roll out dough on a lightly floured board to a 16 X 10 inch rectangle. Transfer to a baking sheet and brush with egg glaze. Bake in heated oven for 15 minutes or until dough starts to brown. Cool slightly, cut in half lengthwise and trim edges. Cool completely on a wire rack.

To make filling: melt chocolate on a heatproof plate over a pan of hot water. Let cool, mix well with other ingredients and spread over unglazed side of one half of dough. Place the other half on top, unglazed side down, and press firmly with a wooden board for 1–2 hours or until filling is firm. Cut into 2 inch squares and store in an airtight container for 1–2 days before eating.

Speculaas
(Dutch Spice Cookies)

½ cup butter
1 cup light brown sugar
1 egg
2 cups flour
½ teaspoon salt
1½ teaspoons ground cinnamon
½ teaspoon ground nutmeg
¼ teaspoon ground white
   pepper
¼ teaspoon ground cloves
2–3 tablespoons milk
   (optional)
30 blanched almonds, split in
   half lengthwise (for
   decoration) – optional
1 tablespoon sugar dissolved
   in little milk (optional)

Wooden cookie or butter mold;
   1½ inch cookie cutter

Makes about 60 cookies.

Method
Oil the mold. Cream butter, add sugar and beat until soft and fluffy. Beat in the egg. Sift flour with salt and spices and stir into the butter mixture. Knead dough until it is smooth, adding a little milk if

it is very stiff. Chill 1 hour or overnight, if you like.

Set oven at moderate (350°F) and oil a baking sheet. Divide dough into balls, press them into the oiled mold and then turn out on baking sheet. Alternatively roll or pat out the dough to ¼ inch thickness, stamp out with the cookie cutter and transfer cookies to the baking sheet. Press half an almond in the center of each cookie, and brush with sugar and milk, if you like.

Bake in heated oven 20–25 minutes for molded cookies or 15–20 minutes for flat cookies, or until they are lightly browned. Store in an airtight container. The flavor mellows if the cookies are kept 2–3 weeks.

American Sugar Cookies

½ cup butter
¾ cup sugar
1 egg, beaten to mix
2 tablespoons milk
1 teaspoon vanilla
grated rind of 1 lemon
2½ cups sifted flour
1 teaspoon baking powder

For decoration
1½ cups glacé icing
colored sugar (for sprinkling)
silver sugar balls
candied cherries, cut in pieces

Fancy shaped cookie cutters (about 3 inch diameter)

Makes 30–35 cookies.

Method
For dough: cream butter, beat in sugar until light and fluffy, then add the egg, milk, vanilla and lemon rind. Beat 2–3 minutes. Sift 2 cups of the flour with the baking powder,

stir into vanilla mixture and add enough of the remaining flour to make a stiff but workable dough. Cover and refrigerate overnight.

Set oven at moderately hot (375°F). Lightly butter and flour a baking sheet.

Divide dough in half and roll out the 2 batches to one-eighth inch thickness. Cut out in fancy shapes with cookie cutters, set on the prepared baking sheet and bake in heated oven 10 minutes or until just beginning to brown. Transfer to a rack and cool.

Spread cookies with glacé icing and sprinkle them with colored sugar or silver balls or decorate with pieces of candied cherry. Store in an airtight container.

Glacé Icing
For 1½ cups: dissolve ¼ cup granulated sugar in ½ cup water over low heat, bring to a boil and simmer 4–5 minutes. Take from heat, and when cold beat 2 cups confectioners' sugar, 1 tablespoon at a time, into the sugar syrup. Stand pan over a pan of hot water until lukewarm; the icing should coat the back of a spoon but still pour easily. Add about 1 tablespoon confectioners' sugar or a little sugar syrup until it is the right consistency.

Caramelized Orange Galette

6 navel oranges
1½ cup quantity puff pastry or puff pastry trimmings
¼ cup shredded almonds
6 tablespoons sugar

Method
Make pastry dough and chill thoroughly. Set oven at hot (425°F).

Roll out the dough or pastry trimmings to a 10-inch circle and trim the edges. Transfer the dough to a baking sheet and chill.

Cut the peel and white pith from the oranges with a serrated-edge knife, using a sawing motion, and cut the oranges in thin slices. Arrange the slices, overlapping closely, on top of the dough round, leaving a narrow border. Scatter almonds on top, then sprinkle thickly with sugar.

Bake the galette in the heated oven for 25–30 minutes or until the almonds are browned and the sugar is lightly caramelized. Transfer galette to a wire rack to cool.

Caramelized orange galette — a puff pastry round is topped with slices of orange and almonds before baking

Chocolate mille feuilles is made with puff pastry and filled with chestnut purée

Sprinkle sieved chestnuts over a layer of whipped cream

Spread melted chocolate and coffee topping over the puff pastry

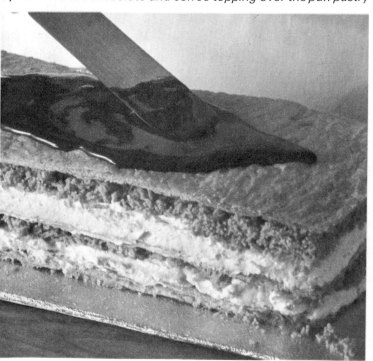

Chocolate Mille Feuilles

1½ cup quantity of puff pastry
  or puff pastry trimmings
¾ lb chestnuts, skinned
2 tablespoons milk
Chantilly cream (made with
  ½ cup heavy cream,
  2–3 teaspoons sugar and a
  few drops of vanilla)

For topping
4 squares (4 oz) semisweet
  chocolate, chopped
2–3 tablespoons strong black
  coffee or water
few drops of oil

Method
Make pastry dough and chill thoroughly.

Set oven at hot (425°F).

Roll out dough (or pastry trimmings) as thinly as possible to a large rectangle, lay on a dampened baking sheet, letting the dough come slightly over the edge, and prick well. Chill 10 minutes and bake in heated oven 10–15 minutes or until brown. Loosen pastry with a metal spatula and turn it over. Bake 5 minutes longer, then transfer to a wire rack to cool.

Simmer the chestnuts, with the milk and water to cover, in a covered pan for 25–30 minutes or until very tender. Drain and work them through a strainer onto a flat platter or tray. Leave until cold – they should be dry and powdery.

Trim edges of pastry and reserve trimmings; cut pastry into 3 even lengths. Spread 1 piece thickly with half the Chantilly cream and sprinkle with half the sieved chestnuts. Press a second piece of pastry lightly on top and repeat the cream and chestnut layer. Gently press the remaining piece of pastry on top.

To make topping: melt chocolate with coffee or water in the top of a double boiler, but do not heat it above luke-warm; it should be the consistency of very thick cream. Add the oil and lightly spread topping over the pastry. Crush the pastry trimmings and sprinkle them in a strip down the long sides of the topping.

Maple Mousse

¾ cup maple syrup
1 envelope gelatin
3 tablespoons cold water
3 egg yolks
2 cups heavy cream, whipped
  until it holds a soft shape
¼ cup shredded almonds (for
  decoration)
1 tablespoon rum

Method
In a cup sprinkle gelatin over the water and let stand 5 minutes or until spongy. Heat the maple syrup in a double boiler, and, when hot, add the softened gelatin and stir until dissolved. Take from heat.

Beat egg yolks until light, add a little hot syrup to them, then stir this mixture back into remaining syrup.

Chill the mixture until cold and fairly stiff, stirring occasionally, and fold in three-quarters of the whipped cream. Pour into a glass bowl and chill at least 2 hours or until set. Sprinkle the top with almonds. Stiffly whip remaining cream, add the rum and serve separately.

Try a simple menu of fruit juice, cold ham and scrambled eggs, croissant and coffee for Sunday breakfast (recipes are on page 78)

WEEKEND MENUS FOR ONE

Cooking for yourself can be boring so here is a collection of simple but lively menus — from Saturday breakfast to Sunday supper — to transform your weekend. Whether you pamper yourself and make all the suggested dishes, or simply pick out one or two of the recipes that appeal to you, you're sure to find cooking easier and more interesting if you follow our guidelines. Our shopping list will also help to make your weekend planning effortless.

There is no better accompaniment to the straightforward, quickly prepared dishes centered on red meats that we suggest here than the no-nonsense wines of the Rhône Valley, sold widely as Côtes du Rhône, or the even more familiar American favorite — California Zinfandel.

This list includes ingredients for all the dishes you plan to make. Pick out what you need for specific dishes.

You will need the following supplies in the cupboard:

1 can consommé
1 small can (8 oz) whole kernel corn
1 small can ripe olives
1 small can (4 oz) pimientoes
1 small can (3 oz) mushrooms
1 large can (1 lb) whole tomatoes
1 small can (6 oz) tomato paste
chicken bouillon cubes
chili powder or cayenne
fresh or frozen chives
oil and olive oil
dry mustard
1 small jar grated Parmesan cheese
pepper, black and white
peppercorns
salt
Tabasco
white wine vinegar
garlic
3–4 onions
1 baking potato
$\frac{1}{2}-\frac{3}{4}$ lb small new potatoes
cereal (optional)
1 box cornstarch
1 small package flour
1 small package long grain rice
1 square (1 oz) unsweetened chocolate
1 package coarsely chopped pecans
jam
1 small box granulated sugar
1 small box brown sugar
almond extract
vanilla extract
$\frac{1}{2}$ cup canned apricots or 1 large ripe peach
canned or frozen fruit juices
little red wine
little white wine (optional)
little rum
little sherry
coffee

You will need the following supplies in the refrigerator:

$\frac{3}{4}$ lb butter
choice of cheese (including Swiss or Cheddar)
1 small carton sour cream
containers of light and heavy cream
6 eggs
1 quart milk
$\frac{1}{4}$ lb scallops
$\frac{1}{4}$ lb fresh or frozen uncooked shrimps
3 slices of cooked ham (includes 2 slices, plus chopped ham for Baked Egg in Tomato)
4 chicken breasts or 4 chicken thighs
2 loin (or rib) lamb chops
$\frac{1}{2}-\frac{3}{4}$ lb Porterhouse, strip or club steak (cut fairly thick)
1 veal kidney
2 croissants or hard rolls
4 flaky dinner rolls or 2 frozen patty shells
1 small loaf bread
gingerbread (ready-made)
1 small can (4 oz) shredded, unsweetened coconut
fresh or frozen green beans
fresh or frozen peas or spinach
2 large tomatoes
1 apple or pear
fresh parsley
fresh mint
head of Boston lettuce
$\frac{1}{4}$ small cucumber
1 lemon
2 ripe bananas
1 grapefruit
fruit for cereal (optional)

SATURDAY BREAKFAST

> *Fruit Juice*
> *or*
> **Half Grapefruit*
> **Baked Egg in Tomato*
> *Coffee*

Grapefruit

To prepare grapefruit half: using a grapefruit knife (or a small sharp knife), remove the core, then cut around edge of the grapefruit between the flesh and pith so flesh is completely detached from the shell. Slip knife down each side of the membranes dividing the grapefruit sections, then lift out all the membranes in 1 piece. Remove any seeds.

Baked Egg in Tomato

1 egg
1 large tomato
1 tablespoon finely chopped onion
little chopped parsley
$\frac{1}{2}$ tablespoon chopped cooked ham (optional)
salt and pepper
1 slice of white bread, crusts removed
$\frac{1}{2}$ tablespoon butter or oil
1 tablespoon grated Swiss or Cheddar cheese

Method
Cut a thin slice from stem end of tomato and scoop out seeds with a teaspoon. Put in onion, parsley, ham, salt and pepper.

Set oven at hot (400°F).

Toast the bread and spread with butter or sprinkle with oil. Place bread in a small oven-proof dish and set tomato on it. Break egg into tomato, sprinkle with grated cheese and bake in heated oven for 12 minutes or until the egg is set and cheese is brown.

SATURDAY LUNCH

> **Shrimps au Gratin*
> *Fresh or Frozen Green Beans*
> *Fresh Fruit*

Shrimps au Gratin

$\frac{1}{4}$ lb uncooked, peeled shrimps
$\frac{1}{4}$ lb scallops
2 tablespoons butter
$\frac{1}{4}$ cup sherry
squeeze of lemon juice
2 teaspoons flour
$\frac{1}{2}$ cup milk
salt and pepper
1 tablespoon grated Parmesan cheese (for sprinkling)

To serve
fresh or frozen green beans
1 tablespoon butter
black pepper, freshly ground

Method
Set oven at moderate (350°F).

Melt half the butter in a pan, put in shrimps and scallops and sauté very lightly for 1–2 minutes or just long enough to heat shellfish thoroughly. Pour on sherry and cook until reduced by half. Add lemon juice. Transfer mixture to a small gratin or ovenproof dish and reserve.

Melt remaining butter in the pan, stir in flour until smooth and blend in milk off the heat. Season, bring to a boil, stirring constantly, and simmer 2 minutes. Spoon sauce over shrimp and scallop mixture. Sprinkle the top with Parmesan cheese and bake in heated oven for 10–12 minutes or until browned. Alternatively, place dish under the broiler for 3–4 minutes or until browned.

Cook fresh green beans in boiling, salted water, uncovered, for 15 minutes or until tender; cook frozen beans according to package directions. Drain well, return to pan with the butter and freshly ground black pepper. Toss beans over low heat until butter melts and serve separately.

Note: Starred recipes in the weekend menus are given in this feature

SATURDAY DINNER

Marinated Steak with Piquant Sauce

Baked Potato with Sour Cream & Chives

Baked Bananas

Marinated Steak
with Piquant Sauce

$\frac{1}{2}-\frac{3}{4}$ lb Porterhouse, strip or club steak

For marinade
2 teaspoons tomato paste
$\frac{1}{2}$ clove of garlic, crushed with a little salt
bouquet garni
6 peppercorns, crushed
1 tablespoon oil
2 tablespoons red wine

For piquant sauce
1 small onion, finely chopped
1 tablespoon oil
$\frac{1}{2}$ cup canned whole tomatoes, crushed (reserve rest of can for lamb chops on Sunday)
1 chicken bouillon cube, dissolved in $\frac{1}{4}$ cup boiling water
dash of Tabasco
large pinch of chili powder or cayenne
salt and pepper
1 slice of canned pimiento, drained and chopped

Method
Combine ingredients for marinade, pour over steak, cover and let stand for several hours, turning occasionally.

To make piquant sauce: fry onion in oil until golden. Add tomatoes, bouillon and nearly all the marinade from the steak. Stir in Tabasco, chili powder or cayenne and seasoning and simmer sauce for about 5 minutes or until it looks pulpy. Stir in pimiento, taste for seasoning and set aside.

Heat broiler 15 minutes before you are ready to eat. Broil the steak, allowing 5–6 minutes for rare steak. Baste with reserved marinade during broiling.

To serve, cut steak in diagonal slices. Combine any meat juices left in broiler pan with the piquant sauce, reheat and spoon over the steak. Serve with a hot baked potato with sour cream and chives.

Baked Potato
with Sour Cream and Chives

1 baking potato
salt
2 tablespoons sour cream mixed with 1 teaspoon chopped chives

Method
Set oven at moderate (350°F).

Wash potato, rub with salt, prick it with a skewer or fork and bake in heated oven for 1–1$\frac{1}{4}$ hours or until tender when pierced with a skewer.

Cut open the top of the potato to let steam escape and spoon over the sour cream and chives mixture.

Baked Bananas

2 bananas
1 small can (4 oz) shredded unsweetened coconut
$\frac{1}{2}$ cup boiling water
1 tablespoon rum
1 tablespoon brown sugar

Method
Put shredded coconut in a bowl, pour on the boiling water and let stand 30 minutes.

Set oven at moderately hot (375°F).

Strain coconut mixture through a piece of cheesecloth, squeezing the coconut thoroughly to extract all the 'milk'. Peel bananas and slice them into a small ovenproof dish. Sprinkle the rum on top and add the coconut milk.

Sprinkle with brown sugar and bake bananas in heated oven for 20 minutes or until browned. Serve hot.

Serve deliciously hot baked bananas with rum for a tempting dessert

SUNDAY BREAKFAST

Cold Ham and Scrambled Eggs

2 slices of cooked ham
2 eggs
large pinch of salt
pinch of pepper
1 tablespoon light cream
2 tablespoons butter
slice of hot buttered toast
  (optional)

Method

Beat eggs in a bowl with a fork until well mixed but not frothy and add seasoning, cream and 1 tablespoon butter in small pieces. Melt remaining butter in a pan or skillet, add egg mixture and cook over low heat. Stir mixture with a wooden spoon or tablespoon, lifting eggs in large creamy flakes as they set. Do not stir eggs rapidly or they will be grainy rather than smooth and creamy.

Watchpoint: remove pan from heat just before mixture has set to the stage you like. The eggs will continue to cook from the heat of the pan.

Arrange ham on a plate. Put eggs on a slice of buttered toast, if you like, or spoon onto the plate and serve with a croissant or hard rolls.

SUNDAY LUNCH

Lamb Chops
with Corn and Tomatoes

2 loin or rib lamb chops
1 can (8 oz) whole kernel corn, drained
rest of tomatoes left over from Saturday dinner
2 tablespoons butter
salt and pepper
1 tablespoon heavy cream or sour cream
1 teaspoon fresh or frozen chopped chives

Method

To broil chops: heat the broiler, spread chops with half the butter and broil 4—5 minutes on each side; seasoning after turning.

To pan fry: heat a heavy skillet or frying pan, add half the butter and when very hot put in chops. Cook over high heat for 3—4 minutes on each side; add seasoning after turning the chops.

Watchpoint: turn chops with 2 spoons to avoid pricking them and losing juices.

Meanwhile, melt remaining butter in a pan, add corn to one side of pan and spoon in tomatoes on other side. Season and heat.

Just before serving, add cream to corn; sprinkle vegetables with chopped chives. Reheat for 1 minute and serve with chops.

Alternative entrée

Chicken Pie Niçoise

2 chicken breasts or thighs
4 flaky dinner rolls or
  2 frozen patty shells
2 cups chicken stock, made from 1 chicken bouillon cube dissolved in 2 cups water
beaten egg (to glaze)

For filling
6 tablespoons heavy cream
1 onion, thinly sliced
1 tablespoon olive oil (for frying)
1 large firm tomato, peeled and thickly sliced
6—8 ripe olives, pitted
salt and pepper

5—6 inch pie pan, or individual ovenproof dish (2—3 cup capacity)

Method

Defrost the patty shells if using. Set oven at hot (400°F).

Simmer chicken breasts or thighs, covered, in stock for 25—30 minutes or until tender. Cool in the liquid. Remove any chicken bones, cut meat into small pieces and arrange in pie pan or dish; pour in the cream.

Fry onion in olive oil until golden, add tomato and olives, season well and cook over fairly high heat for 2—3 minutes, stirring frequently. Spoon this mixture over the chicken and let stand until cool.

Roll out patty shells or flaky rolls into a 5—6 inch circle and cover pie pan or dish. Brush with beaten egg to glaze and bake in heated oven for 15—20 minutes or until well browned. Serve hot with a green vegetable.

Alternative dessert

Apricot or Peach Flip

$\frac{1}{2}$ cup canned apricots (drained), or 1 large ripe peach (pitted)
$\frac{3}{4}$ cup milk
$\frac{1}{2}$ cup cracked ice
dash of almond extract
sprig of mint (to serve)

Method

In a blender combine all the ingredients except mint at high speed until very smooth. Pour into a tumbler and decorate with a sprig of mint.

Note: starred recipes in the weekend menus are given in this feature.

Lunch for one — broiled lamb chops with corn and tomatoes, followed by gingerbread with cheese and apple

SUNDAY SUPPER

Simple Madrilène Soup
or
Lettuce & Cucumber Salad

Chicken with Rice & Mushrooms
or
Veal Kidneys Robert
Fondant Potatoes

Brownie Cake

Simple Madrilène Soup

1 can consommé
1 teaspoon tomato paste
2 tablespoons sherry
2 tablespoons sour cream

Method
Put tomato paste in a saucepan, work in the sherry with a wooden spoon until smooth and add the consommé. Heat gently until very hot and stir in the sour cream; do not boil.

Alternative appetizer

Lettuce and Cucumber Salad

leaves of Boston lettuce, washed and dried
¼ cucumber, thinly sliced

For dressing
1½ teaspoons white wine vinegar
salt and pepper
pinch of dry mustard
2 tablespoons oil

Method
Put lettuce and cucumber slices in a bowl.

To make dressing: mix vinegar with salt, pepper and mustard and whisk in the oil until well blended. Pour over salad and toss.

Watchpoint: dress salad just before serving or the lettuce will become limp.

Chicken with Rice and Mushrooms

2 chicken breasts or thighs
6 tablespoons rice
1 small can (3 oz) sliced mushrooms
2 cups chicken stock made from 1 bouillon cube dissolved in 2 cups water
salt and pepper
1½ teaspoons cornstarch
2–3 tablespoons heavy cream

Method
Put the chicken in a pan with stock and bring slowly to a boil. Cover pan and cook over low heat for 25–30 minutes or until the chicken is tender.

Cook rice in plenty of boiling salted water for 12 minutes or until tender. Drain and rinse with hot water.

Spread in a small buttered ovenproof dish and keep warm in a low oven (300°F).

When chicken is tender, lift out, discard skin and put chicken in a small dish; cover and keep warm. Reserve 1 cup stock from cooking liquid.

Mix cornstarch with the cream, add a little of the reserved hot stock and stir this into the remaining cup of stock. Bring sauce to a boil, stirring until it thickens, then simmer for about 3 minutes. Drain mushrooms, add them to sauce and taste for seasoning. Pour sauce over chicken and serve rice separately. Accompany with a green vegetable like peas or spinach.

Alternative entrée

Veal Kidneys Robert

1 veal kidney
1 tablespoon butter
salt and pepper
1 teaspoon flour
⅓ cup white wine or stock
½ teaspoon prepared mustard
1 teaspoon chopped parsley
squeeze of lemon juice

Method
Skin the kidney. Melt butter in a sauté pan or skillet. Put in kidney, whole, season and fry over medium heat until browned on all sides. Reduce heat slightly and cook gently for 7–10 minutes. Take from heat, slice kidney, cut out the core and keep hot.

Stir flour into pan, pour in wine or stock, bring to a boil and simmer 1–2 minutes. Take from heat and add mustard, parsley and lemon juice, season to taste and replace kidney with its juice. Heat mixture but do not boil. Serve with fondant potatoes.

Fondant Potatoes

Scrub or peel ⅓–½ lb small new potatoes, rinse and dry them. In a skillet or shallow flameproof casserole melt 1 tablespoon butter, add the whole potatoes and cover. Cook over moderate heat, shaking pan from time to time to turn potatoes; do not lift lid for the first 10–15 minutes as steam helps potatoes to cook more quickly and prevents them from sticking. Prick potatoes with a skewer and, if they are not tender, continue cooking a few more minutes. Sprinkle with salt just before serving. Serves 1.

Brownie Cake

1 square (1 oz) unsweetened chocolate
3 tablespoons butter
½ cup sugar
1 egg
½ teaspoon vanilla
6 tablespoons flour
¼ teaspoon salt
¼ cup coarsely chopped pecans

6 inch foil pie pan

Method
Butter pie pan and set oven at moderately hot (375°F).

In a saucepan over a pan of hot water, melt butter with chocolate, stirring until smooth. Take from heat, then stir in sugar, egg, vanilla, flour, salt and pecans until mixture is smooth. Pour into prepared pan and bake in heated oven for 35–40 minutes or until cake shrinks slightly from sides; cool in pan. Turn out cake before serving.

Homey madrilène soup is flavored with sherry and tomato

MIDDLE EASTERN COOKING

Middle Eastern cooking covers a much wider area than just Turkey, Syria, Iraq, Jordan, the Lebanon, Israel and Egypt. At its zenith, the Ottoman Empire of the Turks stretched from Central Europe, all around the eastern and southern shores of the Mediterranean to Morocco and the Turks took their cooking traditions with them. The same traditions remain today, mingled with native cooking styles and adapted in different countries to suit local ingredients and tastes, but with the same distinctive base.

The cooking and serving of food is particularly important to Middle Eastern Muslims who regard hospitality as the highest of virtues. The Middle Eastern staple meat is lamb, and goat is often eaten too. Older lambs and sheep are cut up for a variety of stews including Greek moussaka — made with ground lamb, Syrian kibbeh — ground lamb pounded with cracked wheat, and the cous-cous of North Africa — a stew of lamb and vegetables steamed with a coarse semolina. Shish kebab is universal, usually made with cubes of lamb interspersed with pieces of onion, bay leaves, green peppers and tomatoes and other ingredients according to the country. For a special feast, smaller lambs are filled with an aromatic stuffing and roasted whole on a spit, preferably over charcoal.

The scorching summer climate of all Middle Eastern and North African countries makes keeping fresh food a problem so milk and butter are generally replaced by yogurt and fresh cheese. Every household makes its own tart, refreshing yogurt with cow's or goat's milk that may be served plain with bread for breakfast or as a snack, diluted with water as a drink, or used in cooking savory and sweet dishes.

Vegetables are of good quality but limited to staples like eggplant, tomatoes, green peppers, and cucumbers. Onions of all kinds are immensely popular and garlic is added to almost all meat, vegetables and salads in light or lavish quantities.

In areas with a Mediterranean climate, olives and figs are so plentiful that the olive branch and fig tree have become symbols of contentment and peace; in some other areas fresh dates grow in abundance. The seeds of the pomegranate are used to garnish soups, salads and mixed with ground meat; the juice alone is enjoyed as a breakfast drink.

These are the lands of the lemon and its juice is a favorite flavoring for savory dishes; used as we would vinegar, lemon juice adds a pleasant aromatic flavor that is typically Middle Eastern. The use of spices is common — cumin, saffron, coriander, cloves and cinnamon are added to savory dishes as well as desserts.

The invariable opening to any meal is a selection of appetizers — these may range from a dish of olives, a few tomatoes and a bowl of yogurt ▶

served with bread to an array of literally dozens of dips. Hummus (chick-pea purée), baba ghanouj (eggplant purée), dolmas (stuffed vine leaves), are popular, as are stuffed baby eggplants, pickled vegetables, fresh salads, and tiny meatballs — all served with freshly baked pita bread.

The Middle East is renowned for its sweet, melting pastries. Many of them are based on phyllo — tissue-thin pastry sheets that are layered with melted butter or oil and baked in a wide variety of crisp flaky shapes. Phyllo is often filled with nuts and soaked in honey or sugar syrup; it is used for savory dishes, too, like Greek spanakopita and Moroccan bistaela.

Middle Eastern cookies are equally characteristic — melting, sugary delicacies often made with nuts and flavored with spices. Fruits are usually eaten fresh or, in winter, as jam or compote. Iced fruit drinks, overly sweetened by Western standards, are enormously popular. They are called 'sharbah' and are the forerunner of our sherbet.

Mint tea, iced in summer, hot in winter, is the most popular of several herb infusions and strong thick Turkish coffee, with sugar, is served with ceremony to all guests when they enter the house; it is a mandatory opening to business meetings.

Alcohol is forbidden to orthodox Muslims but this does not restrict the popularity of arak and ouzo — fiery, anise-flavored liquors — and several countries make considerable quantities of wine.

Our **Cooking Consultant** on **Middle Eastern Cooking, Elizabeth Naltchayan,** was born in Lebanon of Turkish parents. Mrs. Naltchayan, fluent in Armenian, Arabic, French and Turkish, has traveled extensively in the Middle East and Europe, and now lives in Virginia.

Middle Eastern Ingredients

Phyllo — tissue paper-thin sheets of pastry — comes in 1 lb packages. Excellent commercial brands are available in Middle Eastern and Greek markets.

Yogurt is always freshly made in the Middle East and tastes quite different from our commercial product. In Jordan it is called laban, in Greece yaourti and in Turkey yoghurt. The nearest substitute for Middle Eastern yogurt is the kind available at health food stores; otherwise use plain commercial yogurt.

Couscous, a coarse-grained semolina made from coarsely ground wheat, is steamed over a broth or stew.

Sesame oil, extracted from the seeds of the sesame plant, is widely used.

Tahina (sesame paste) is made from sesame seed crushed to a smooth paste. This has a nut-like flavor that blends well with chick-peas, avocado and eggplant.

Cracked wheat (bulghour, burghul, or bulgur) is made by boiling and drying grains of wheat. It is often added to soups and stuffings and can be made into a pilaf.

Orange flower water is made from the flowers of the bitter orange tree, that grows the Seville oranges from which some types of marmalade are made. Orange flower water is used for flavoring many cakes and pastries.

APPETIZERS

Cacik
(Yogurt soup)

2 cups plain yogurt
1 medium cucumber, peeled
1–2 cloves of garlic, crushed
1 tablespoon chopped fresh mint
salt and white pepper

This soup is served as a refreshing appetizer in Turkey. If possible, use tart goats' milk yogurt or, when this is unobtainable, sharpen the soup by adding 1 tablespoon of white vinegar.

Method
Cut the cucumber in half lengthwise, scoop out the seeds with a teaspoon, and grate the cucumber flesh. Pile it in a colander, sprinkle it with a little salt and let stand 30 minutes to draw out the juices (dégorger).

Mix the garlic (adjust quantities to your taste) with a little of the yogurt. Stir this into the remaining yogurt with the grated cucumber, half the mint and salt and white pepper to taste. Cover the soup and chill thoroughly. Serve in bowls sprinkled with the remaining chopped mint.

Harira
(Moroccan Soup with Lentils)

1 cup ($\frac{1}{2}$ lb) dried Egyptian lentils, soaked overnight and drained
salt
juice of 2 lemons
$\frac{1}{4}$ cup butter
1 lb lamb or veal bones
$\frac{1}{2}$ lb lean lamb or veal, cut in cubes
large pinch of saffron, soaked in $\frac{1}{4}$ cup boiling water for 30 minutes
2 quarts water
pepper
12–16 baby onions, peeled
8 tomatoes, peeled, seeded and chopped
few sprigs of fresh Italian parsley (coriander)
few sprigs of parsley
$\frac{1}{4}$ cup flour

Serves 6–8.

Method

Put the lentils in a pan with water to cover, add the lid and simmer 1–1½ hours until tender; add salt halfway through cooking. Drain and sprinkle with the juice of ½ lemon and dot with 2 tablespoons butter.

Meanwhile roast the lamb or veal bones in a very hot oven (500°F) or until slightly charred. Put the bones in a pan with the lamb or veal meat, saffron, 1 quart water and seasoning and simmer 1 hour. Add the onions and simmer 30 minutes longer or until onions and meat are tender. Discard the bones.

In a kettle simmer the tomatoes with the remaining quart of water and seasoning for 15 minutes. Stir in the lentils and the meat mixture with its liquid.

Finely chop the two kinds of parsley and pound in a mortar and pestle or purée the parsley in a blender with a little liquid from the soup. Stir about ½ cup liquid into the flour to form a smooth paste.

Bring the soup to a boil, stir in the flour paste and cook until thickened. Stir in the lemon juice and remaining butter and taste for seasoning.

Moroccan lentil soup is served in a cooking pot called a tajine. Melon seeds are served on the side

Assorted appetizers include from left: kibbeh nayya (ground lamb with bulgur), and pita (bread) above; in the center, salata (mixed salad) and hummus bi tahina (chick-peas with sesame paste) above; scallions, feta cheese and ripe olives below; on the right, dolmas (stuffed vine leaves); olives. All these are served with pita

Dolmas
(Stuffed Vine Leaves)

1 jar (8 oz) vine leaves in brine
½ cup rice
½ lb ground lamb or beef
1 tomato, peeled, seeded and chopped
1 onion, finely chopped
1 clove of garlic, crushed
salt and pepper
juice of 2 lemons
2 tablespoons olive oil
1–1½ cups water

To serve
1 lemon, cut in wedges
½ cup plain yogurt

Dolma in Turkish means 'stuffed' and many stuffed vegetables can be called dolmas though the name has come to be associated mainly with vine leaves. Vine leaves may be filled with ground meat and served hot, or served cold, when the meat is usually though not always omitted.

Method
Drain the vine leaves, put them in a large bowl and pour plenty of boiling water over them, separating the leaves as much as possible; let soak 20–30 minutes. Drain the leaves, cover them with cold water, then lift them out one by one and drain again on paper towels.

In a bowl mix the rice, ground meat, tomato, onion and garlic with plenty of pepper and a little salt. Work the mixture with the hand for 1 minute. With a vine leaf, vein side up, set a tablespoon of filling on top, fold over the edges of the leaf and roll it to form a cylindrical parcel; squeeze lightly to seal. Repeat until all the filling is used and a few leaves are left.

Lay the remaining leaves in a shallow saucepan to prevent dolmas from sticking, and pack the dolmas into the pan tightly so they cannot unroll. Sprinkle with lemon juice and olive oil, pour over the water, cover the pan tightly and simmer 1 hour or until the dolmas are firm and the rice is cooked. If the pan gets dry during cooking, add a little more water. Serve the dolmas hot with lemon wedges and yogurt.
Note: if serving dolmas cold; omit meat from recipe and add ½ cup more rice and ¼ teaspoon each of ground cinnamon and allspice to the stuffing.

Baba Ghanouj (Eggplant with Sesame Oil)

1 medium eggplant
2 cloves of garlic, crushed
juice of 2 lemons
$\frac{1}{4}$ cup sesame oil
1 tablespoon chopped parsley
salt

For garnish
1 tablespoon sesame oil
3 scallions, thinly sliced

Method

If possible grill the eggplant over charcoal, turning it constantly for about 20 minutes or until the skin is charred and the flesh is tender. Charcoal gives the eggplant an excellent flavor, but it can also be held over a gas flame or broiled 4–5 inches from the element of an electric broiler.

When cooked, peel the eggplant under cold water, discarding any charred flesh. Crush the flesh to a purée and beat in the garlic and lemon juice, then beat in the sesame oil, a little at a time. Alternatively, purée the eggplant in a blender with the lemon juice and garlic and gradually beat in the oil. Add the parsley to the purée with salt to taste and pile in a bowl. Sprinkle the top with sesame oil and sliced scallions.

Kibbeh

Kibbeh is the hamburger of Syria and Lebanon. It is seasoned and served in many different ways but the basis is always ground meat and a grain, usually cracked wheat (bulgur).

Kibbeh Nayya (Ground Lamb with Bulgur)

1 lb ground lean loin or leg of lamb
$\frac{3}{4}$ cup fine cracked wheat (bulgur)
1 large onion, grated
1–2 tablespoons cold water
salt
black pepper, freshly ground

For serving
1 tablespoon olive oil
1 scallion, finely sliced

Method

Pound the meat in a mortar and pestle until it draws away from the sides of the bowl. Add the onion and continue pounding, adding 1–2 tablespoons cold water, until the mixture is very smooth. Alternatively work the lamb, onion and water several times through the fine blade of a grinder, then beat the mixture until smooth.

Rinse the bulgur in a sieve with cold water, squeeze it to drain and work into the lamb mixture with plenty of salt and pepper to taste. If the mixture is not smooth and fine-textured, pass it again several times through the grinder. Pile the kibbeh on a plate in a smooth mound and sprinkle it with olive oil and sliced scallion.

Broiled or Fried Kibbeh

Make mixture as for kibbeh nayya and shape into round patties about 2 inches diameter and $\frac{1}{2}$ inch thick. In a skillet heat $\frac{1}{2}$ cup olive oil and fry the patties for 4–5 minutes on each side or until they are golden brown and no longer pink in the center.

Alternatively broil the patties 5–6 minutes on each side until browned and cooked through.

Kibbeh bi Sanieh (Baked Kibbeh)

1 lb quantity kibbeh nayya

For filling
$\frac{1}{2}$ lb coarsely ground lean leg of lamb
$\frac{1}{2}$ cup pine nuts
1 medium onion, finely chopped
2 tablespoons oil
salt
black pepper, freshly ground
$\frac{1}{4}$ teaspoon ground cinnamon
$\frac{1}{4}$ teaspoon ground allspice
$\frac{1}{2}$ cup melted butter (for topping)

12 X 9 inch cake pan or baking dish

Method

To make the filling: fry the onion in the oil until golden brown. Add the lamb and pine nuts and cook, stirring to break up the meat, until the lamb has no trace of pink and the nuts are browned. Take from heat, pour off any excess fat and stir in the spices with plenty of salt and pepper to taste.

Butter the cake pan or baking dish and spread half the kibbeh nayya in it, pressing it down lightly. Spread the filling evenly on top, then add the remaining ground lamb mixture. Pour the melted butter on top and bake in a moderate oven (350°F) for $\frac{3}{4}$–1 hour or until the top is browned and crisp and the kibbeh is no longer pink. Cut in squares or diamonds and serve hot or cold.

Hummus bi Tahina (Chick-peas with Sesame Paste)

$\frac{3}{4}$ cup dried chick-peas, soaked overnight and drained
juice of 2 lemons (or to taste)
$\frac{3}{4}$ cup tahina (sesame paste)
2–3 cloves of garlic, crushed
salt

For garnish
1 teaspoon paprika
parsley sprigs (optional)

Method

Put the chick-peas in a pan with cold water to cover, bring to a boil and simmer, covered, for 1–1$\frac{1}{2}$ hours or until very tender. Drain well, reserving the cooking liquid, work chick-peas through a sieve or food mill, and beat in the lemon juice with enough cooking liquid to make a smooth paste. Alternatively purée the chick-peas in a blender with the lemon juice and a little cooking liquid. Gradually beat in the tahina, then add the garlic and season to taste with salt. The mixture should be firm enough to hold its shape but thin enough to spread easily.

Pile the hummus on a plate, sprinkle with paprika and garnish with parsley sprigs, if you like. Serve with pita (see page 88).

Falafel
(Chick-pea Balls)

2 cups dried chick-peas, soaked overnight and drained
2 red or Bermuda onions, very finely chopped
$\frac{1}{2}$ teaspoon crushed red pepper
1 teaspoon ground cumin
1 teaspoon ground coriander
2 cloves of garlic, crushed
salt and pepper
juice of 1 lemon
deep fat (for frying)

Falafel are small deep fried balls of chick-pea mixture that are served with hot pita bread, taratoor dressing and a salad such as mixed salad. They are practically Egypt's national dish and are also popular in Israel where they are stuffed into the pita with a few spoons of salad and sold by street vendors. Makes 20–22 falafel.

Method
Put the chick-peas in a saucepan with water to cover, bring to a boil and simmer, covered, for 1–1$\frac{1}{2}$ hours or until very tender. Drain them. Mix chick-peas with the onion, red pepper, cumin, coriander, garlic, and salt and pepper and work the mixture twice through the fine blade of a grinder. Beat in the lemon juice to form a coarse purée and taste for seasoning. Alternatively, purée all the ingredients in the blender and taste for seasoning.

Cover the mixture and let stand 30 minutes.

Wet the palms of your hands and roll the mixture into balls the size of a large walnut and let stand 30–45 minutes.

Heat the fat to 375°F on a fat thermometer. Place half the balls in a frying basket, lower them into the hot fat and fry until golden brown.

Drain on paper towels. Fry the remaining balls and serve hot with pita bread and salata (mixed salad).

Salata
(Mixed Salad with Taratoor Dressing)

1 cucumber, peeled, seeds removed and diced
2 tomatoes, peeled, seeded and diced
3–4 scallions, trimmed and thickly sliced
1 green pepper, cored, seeded and diced
taratoor dressing (see right)
parsley sprigs (for garnish)

Method
Sprinkle the cucumber lightly with salt, let stand 30 minutes to draw out juices (dégorger), then rinse and dry on paper towels.

Mix the cucumber, tomato, scallion and green pepper, toss with the taratoor dressing and pile on a platter. Serve within 2 hours or the vegetables will become limp. Garnish with parsley sprigs just before serving.

Feta is a white cheese traditionally made by the shepherds in the mountains near Athens from goats' or ewes' milk.

Slightly astringent and salty, it is used in Greek cheese pastries and is also good in salads.

Taratoor Dressing

2–3 cloves of garlic, crushed
$\frac{1}{2}$ cup tahina (sesame paste)
juice of 2 lemons
$\frac{1}{4}$–$\frac{1}{3}$ cup water
$\frac{1}{2}$ teaspoon ground cumin
salt

Method
Beat garlic into tahina, then gradually beat in lemon juice and enough cold water to make a smooth creamy dressing. Add cumin and salt to taste.

Pita
(Arab bread)

1 package dry or 1 cake compressed yeast
about 1$\frac{1}{4}$ cups lukewarm water
3 cups flour
pinch of salt
pinch of sugar
1 tablespoon olive oil

Makes 6 breads.

Method
Sprinkle the yeast over $\frac{1}{4}$ cup of the lukewarm water and let stand 5 minutes or until dissolved. Sift the flour, salt and sugar into a warm bowl, make a well in the center and add the yeast mixture with the remaining water and olive oil. Gradually work in the flour with your hand, adding more water, if necessary, to make a smooth soft dough. Turn out on a floured board and knead until the dough is smooth and elastic. Replace it in the bowl, cover with a cloth and let rise in a warm place for 1–1$\frac{1}{2}$ hours or until doubled in bulk.

Work the dough lightly to knock out the air, divide it into 6 pieces and flatten each piece with your hand or a rolling pin to 10 inch rounds, each $\frac{1}{4}$ inch thick. Set rounds on baking sheets, cover with a cloth and let rise in a warm place for 20 minutes.

Set oven at very hot (450°F). Place the bread on the lowest shelf of the oven and bake 10 minutes or until lightly browned and puffed around the edges with a slight hollow in the center. Repeat with remaining bread rounds and serve as soon as possible.

Taramasalata

1 jar (8 oz) tarama
juice of 1 lemon
3 slices of bread, crusts removed
$\frac{1}{2}$ cup water
1 cup olive oil
black pepper, freshly ground
2 tablespoons chopped parsley

Tarama is salted fish roe in oil; it is available in Middle Eastern and specialty food stores.

Method
Beat tarama with lemon juice until smooth. Soak the bread in the water and tear it into pieces with 2 forks.

Beat soaked bread into tarama, then gradually add olive oil, beating constantly. Continue beating until tarama is light colored and soft in consistency.

Add pepper to taste and beat in parsley. If you like, taramasalata can be made in the blender. It may be made 1–2 days before serving, and kept, covered, in refrigerator.

Serve chilled with hot pita, toast or unsalted crackers.

MAIN DISHES

Classic Moussaka

1½ lb ground lean lamb
3 medium eggplants
about ½ cup olive oil
2 onions, thinly sliced
1 clove of garlic, crushed
2 tomatoes, peeled, seeded and chopped
1 cup tomato purée
½ teaspoon ground allspice
1 teaspoon basil
1 tablespoon chopped parsley
salt
black pepper, freshly ground

For topping
3 tablespoons butter
3 tablespoons flour
3 cups milk
3 eggs
pinch of nutmeg
½ cup grated Parmesan cheese (for sprinkling) – optional

Baking dish or casserole (2½ – 3½ inches deep)

The Greeks take credit for moussaka but innumerable versions are found throughout the Middle East, some containing potato, or using zucchini instead of eggplant. In some elaborate recipes, the lamb is molded inside eggplant skins instead of layering all the ingredients together in a baking dish.

Method
Cut the eggplants in fairly thin slices, discarding the stems and place them on oiled baking sheets. Brush the slices with olive oil and bake in a moderate oven (350°F) for 15 minutes or until beginning to brown. Turn over, brush again with oil and continue baking 10–15 minutes or until browned and tender.

In a large skillet heat 2 tablespoons olive oil and fry the onion until browned. Add the ground lamb and cook, stirring, until browned. Add the garlic, tomatoes, tomato purée, allspice, herbs and seasoning. Stir well and simmer 15 minutes or until the liquid is well reduced and the mixture is thick. Taste for seasoning – the mixture should be highly seasoned.

Grease the baking dish or casserole, arrange a layer of baked eggplant slices in the bottom and add a layer of meat mixture. Continue making layers, ending with a layer of eggplant.

To make the topping: in a saucepan melt the butter, stir in the flour and pour in the milk, off the heat. Bring to a boil, stirring, and simmer 2 minutes. Take from the heat, beat in the eggs, one by one, and season well, adding the nutmeg. Pour the topping over the moussaka and sprinkle with cheese, if you like. Bake in a moderate oven (350°F) for ¾–1 hour or until the moussaka is well browned and bubbling at the edges. Cut in squares to serve.

Tiropita (Greek Cheese Pie)

Line a pan or dish with 1 package (1 lb) phyllo pastry as for Greek spinach pie (see right) and fill it with 1½ lb crumbled feta cheese, beaten until mixed with 4 eggs and 1 cup milk; season the filling to taste with white pepper and a pinch of nutmeg (salt is not needed). Complete; bake and serve as for spinach pie.

Spanakopita (Greek Spinach Pie)

1 lb package phyllo pastry
2 lb fresh spinach, well washed, drained, stems removed and finely chopped
¼ cup olive oil
5–6 scallions, trimmed and finely sliced
2 eggs, beaten to mix
½ lb feta cheese, crumbled
¼ cup chopped fresh dill or 2 tablespoons dried dill
2 tablespoons chopped parsley
salt
black pepper, freshly ground
4–6 tablespoons olive oil (for brushing)

13 X 9 inch roasting pan or baking dish

Serves 6–8 people.

Method
Heat ¼ cup olive oil in a skillet and fry the scallions until soft but not browned. Stir in the spinach, cover tightly and cook very gently for 2–3 minutes until the spinach is wilted. Remove the lid and cook the spinach, stirring constantly, until the moisture has evaporated. Take from the heat, let cool and stir in the beaten eggs, feta cheese, dill, parsley and salt and pepper to taste.

Set the oven at moderate (350°F) and brush the cake pan or dish with olive oil. Line the pan with half the phyllo pastry sheets, brushing each sheet, including the sides, with olive oil and pressing the sheets well into the corners and on the sides. Spread the spinach mixture evenly over the pastry and top with the remaining sheets, again brushing each one with oil. Press the sheets firmly together at the edges of the pie and trim with a sharp knife. Brush the top with olive oil and bake in the heated oven for 30 minutes. Reduce the heat to low (300°F) and continue baking 30 minutes or until golden brown. Cool slightly, then cut into squares and serve hot or at room temperature.

For Greek spinach pie, spoon the spinach and feta cheese mixture into the pan lined with phyllo pastry, then top with remaining sheets of pastry

To Use Phyllo Pastry

Unroll the sheets and cover with a slightly dampened cloth. Keep them covered while you are working – if left in the air, they dry quickly and disintegrate; if too damp, they stick together.

Peel off sheets, one by one, and use them as described in the individual recipe. Once opened, the pastry should be shaped within a few hours. Once shaped, dishes can be wrapped tightly and frozen ready for baking.

Greek lamb stew is served over currant and pistachio pilaf

Imam Bayeldi
(Turkish Fainting Imam)

2 medium eggplants
salt
5 tablespoons olive oil
about 1 cup water
juice of 1 lemon
pinch of sugar

For filling
3 tablespoons olive oil
3 medium onions, finely chopped
3 cloves of garlic, crushed
3 tomatoes, peeled, seeded and chopped
2 tablespoons chopped parsley
salt
black pepper, freshly ground

No one knows if the Imam fainted with pleasure from the richness of this eggplant dish or with horror at the cost of the ingredients (though it is not expensive to make here).

Method
Cut the stems from the eggplants, then with a vegetable peeler peel off the skin in $\frac{3}{4}$–1 inch strips, leaving the skin between. Cut each eggplant almost in half lengthwise, leaving it joined at one side. Sprinkle all the cut surfaces with salt and let stand 30 minutes to draw out the bitter juices (dégorger). Rinse the eggplants and pat dry with paper towels.

For the filling: in a skillet heat 3 tablespoons oil and fry the onion until golden brown. Add the garlic, cook 1 minute, then take from the heat and stir in the tomatoes, parsley and salt and pepper to taste.

Set the eggplants in a casserole, open up the halves and pile the filling inside. Pour over the 5 tablespoons oil,

water, lemon juice and sugar, adding enough water to come three-quarters up the sides of the eggplant. Cover and simmer 1–1$\frac{1}{4}$ hours until the eggplants are very tender and most of the liquid has evaporated. If necessary, remove the lid during the last 15 minutes cooking so the liquid reduces to about $\frac{1}{2}$ cup.

Cool, transfer the eggplants to a serving dish, pour over the cooking juices and serve at room temperature.

Currant and Pistachio Pilaf

1 cup long grain rice
$\frac{3}{4}$ cup currants
$\frac{3}{4}$ cup shelled pistachios
3 tablespoons butter
1 small onion, finely chopped
2 cups chicken stock
salt and pepper

Method
Blanch the pistachios for 1 minute in boiling water, drain and halve them.

In a flameproof casserole melt 2 tablespoons of the butter, add the onion and fry until golden brown. Stir in the rice and cook, stirring, until the grains look transparent. Pour on the stock, season and bring to a boil.

Cover pot and simmer 20 minutes or until all the stock is absorbed and the rice is just tender. Let stand, covered, 10 minutes, then stir in the currants, pistachios, and remaining butter with a fork. Cover and stand in a warm place or heat very gently for 5 minutes. Taste for seasoning and serve.

Arni Kokkinisto
(Greek Lamb Stew)

1$\frac{1}{2}$ lb lean leg or shoulder of lamb, cut in 1$\frac{1}{2}$ inch cubes
2 tablespoons olive oil
2 medium onions, sliced
1 clove of garlic, crushed
2 tablespoons tomato paste
1$\frac{1}{2}$–2 cups beef stock
1 teaspoon ground cumin
1 teaspoon ground allspice
salt and pepper

Method
In a flameproof casserole heat the oil and brown the meat on all sides over fairly high heat, a few pieces at a time. Take out, add the onion and cook until golden brown. Add the garlic and cook 1 minute longer. Stir in the tomato paste, then add 1$\frac{1}{2}$ cups stock, the spices and seasoning; bring to a boil, stirring.

Replace meat, cover and simmer 1–1$\frac{1}{2}$ hours or until the meat is very tender, adding more stock if the mixture seems dry. At the end of cooking, sauce should be well reduced; if necessary, reduce by boiling (after removing the meat), then taste for seasoning.

Arrange meat on a serving dish, spoon over the sauce and pile currant and pistachio pilaf on the dish or serve it separately.

Cut the lamb in cubes for Greek lamb stew

Brown the cubes of meat a few pieces at a time

91

Lamb couscous, made with semolina, is a popular dish in the Middle East. It is made in a couscoussier, the traditional 2-tiered pot. Serve couscous with harissa sauce, and raisins soaked in a little boiling water

Couscous

Couscous – the national dish of Algeria, Tunisia and Morocco – has many variations. Couscous itself is coarse-grained semolina made from coarsely ground wheat; it is steamed over a broth or stew made of lamb, chicken or fish, and vegetables. The skill lies in cooking the couscous so the grains are light and separate. Often chick-peas are added and the broth may be flavored with saffron or tomato. The dish is usually served with a fiery chili sauce (harissa sauce).

Couscous is made in a couscoussier – a 2-tiered pot consisting of a regular pan below for the broth or stew with a coarse sieve fitted above it to hold the couscous for steaming; you can improvise with a large strainer that fits exactly into a deep saucepan. It is important that the couscous grains do not touch the broth.

Lamb Couscous

2 cups (1 lb) couscous
2–2½ lb shoulder of lamb, cut in cubes
3 onions, chopped
3 tomatoes, peeled, seeded and chopped
2 dried red chili peppers
½ cup dried chick-peas, soaked overnight and drained
1½ quarts water
salt and pepper
2 small turnips, quartered
4–5 carrots, cut in ½ inch slices
2 tablespoons butter
2 red bell peppers, peeled, cored and cut in strips
1 medium eggplant, cut in cubes
harissa sauce (for serving)
1 cup raisins (for serving)

Couscoussier

Serves 4–6.

Method
In the bottom of the couscoussier, put the lamb, onions, tomatoes, chili peppers, chick-peas, water and seasoning, cover and simmer 30 minutes.

Meanwhile rinse the couscous in a strainer with cold water, then work the grains little by little between the palms of the hand so they resemble crumbs and do not stick together in lumps. Add turnips and carrots to the lamb mixture and bring to a boil.

Put the upper part of the couscoussier on top and add the couscous a little at a time, waiting for steam to rise between each addition. Where the 2 pans join wrap with a cloth, if necessary, so steam can only escape through the couscous. Simmer 30 minutes, uncovered, stirring the couscous grains occasionally so they cook evenly. Turn the couscous onto a tray, spread out, break up the grains and let stand 10–15 minutes to dry.

Sprinkle couscous with 2–3 tablespoons cold water, add salt, pepper and the butter, cut in small pieces; stir well. Add the bell peppers and eggplant to the bottom of the pan, replace the top of the couscoussier, put back the couscous and simmer 30 minutes longer or until the meat and vegetables are very tender. If the pan gets dry during cooking, add more water. The couscous grains should be separate and light.

Arrange the meat and vegetables in a dish, discarding the dried chili peppers, spoon over some of the cooking liquid and serve the rest separately. Pile the couscous in a separate dish. As an accompaniment, serve with raisins that have soaked in a little boiling water. Serve harissa sauce separately.

Harissa Sauce

8–10 dried red chili peppers
1 teaspoon vinegar
½ teaspoon cayenne
1 teaspoon ground coriander
2 tablespoons olive oil
1 tablespoon boiling water

Method
Wash chilies in cold water, remove the veins, stems and seeds and cut in small pieces. Pour on 1–2 cups boiling water, add the vinegar and let soak about 30 minutes.

Drain peppers and finely chop the pulp. Add the cayenne and coriander to the pulp and gradually beat in the oil to form a smooth mixture. Stir in the boiling water.

Fish Couscous

2 cups (1 lb) couscous
3 lb whole mullet, bass or red snapper, cleaned, scales removed and trimmed, preferably with head left on
1 tablespoon olive oil
1 onion, finely sliced
1 tablespoon tomato paste
$\frac{1}{2}$ cup chick-peas, soaked overnight and drained
$\frac{1}{2}$ lb fish bones (optional)
$1\frac{1}{2}$ quarts water
pinch of saffron, soaked in 2 tablespoons boiling water for 30 minutes
1 teaspoon grated fresh ginger root or $\frac{1}{2}$ teaspoon ground ginger
$\frac{1}{4}$ teaspoon ground cinnamon
1 whole clove
$\frac{1}{4}$ teaspoon ground nutmeg
pinch of cayenne
salt
black pepper, freshly ground
4 medium white turnips, peeled and quartered
4 carrots, peeled and quartered
6–8 small potatoes, peeled
1 stalk of celery, sliced
1 large onion, quartered or 12 baby onions, peeled
2 tablespoons butter
4 zucchini, thickly sliced
$\frac{1}{2}$ cup raisins
$\frac{1}{2}$ cup whole blanched almonds (for garnish)
harissa sauce (for serving) – see page 93

Couscoussier

Serves 6–8 people.

Method
In the bottom of the couscoussier heat the oil and fry the sliced onion until golden brown. Add the tomato paste, drained chick-peas, fish bones (if using), water, saffron and liquid, ginger, cinnamon, clove, nutmeg, cayenne and seasoning. Cover and simmer 45 minutes. Discard the fish bones.

Meanwhile rinse the couscous in a strainer with cold water, then work the grains little by little between the palms of the hands so they resemble crumbs and do not stick together in lumps. Add the turnips, carrots, potatoes, celery and onion to the chick-pea mixture and bring to a boil. Put the upper part of the couscoussier on top and add the couscous a little at a time, waiting for steam to rise between each addition. Wrap where the 2 pans join with a cloth if necessary so steam can only escape through couscous. Simmer 30 minutes, uncovered, stirring couscous grains occasionally so they cook evenly. Turn the couscous onto a tray, spread out and break up the grains and let stand 10–15 minutes to dry.

Sprinkle couscous with 2–3 tablespoons cold water, add salt, pepper and the butter, cut in small pieces; stir well. Add the zucchini and the raisins to the bottom of the pan, set the fish down among the vegetables, replace the top of the couscoussier, put back the couscous and continue simmering 30 minutes or until the fish flakes easily when tested with a fork. If the pan gets dry during cooking, add more water. The couscous grains should be separate and light. Arrange the fish and vegetables in a dish. Spoon over a little of the cooking liquid, and serve the rest separately. Sprinkle the fish with almonds and keep warm. Pile the couscous in a bowl and keep warm. Serve harissa sauce separately.

Bistaela
(Moroccan Chicken Pie)

1 lb package phyllo pastry
4 whole squabs or 3–$3\frac{1}{2}$ lb roasting chicken, cut in pieces
2 cups water
juice of 2 lemons
2 onions, sliced
1 teaspoon ground ginger
large pinch of saffron, soaked in $\frac{1}{4}$ cup boiling water for 30 minutes
3 inch piece of cinnamon stick
1 teaspoon salt
$\frac{1}{2}$ teaspoon pepper
8 eggs, beaten to mix
$\frac{1}{4}$ cup chopped fresh coriander
1 cup melted butter
1 cup slivered almonds, browned and chopped
2 tablespoons sugar
$\frac{1}{2}$ teaspoon ground cinnamon (for sprinkling)

15 X 11 inch jelly roll pan

Moroccan cooks make a pastry very similar to phyllo on round griddles so the pastry sheets are circular. In this recipe, phyllo has been substituted, and the shape of the pie has been changed from round to rectangular to suit the sheets of phyllo.

Method
In a pan combine the whole squabs or chicken pieces, water, lemon juice, onion, ginger, saffron liquid, cinnamon stick and salt and pepper. Cover and simmer 45 minutes or until the squabs or chicken are very tender and fall easily from the bones. Take out the birds, and remove the flesh in large pieces, discarding the bones. Boil the cooking liquid until it is reduced to $1\frac{1}{2}$ cups; discard the cinnamon stick.

Mix the beaten eggs, chopped coriander and a little salt and pepper; add any very small pieces of chicken or squab, then add mixture gradually to cooking liquid, stirring over low heat until the eggs thicken and become scrambled; taste for seasoning and let cool.

Brush jelly roll pan with melted butter. Line it with sheets of pastry as follows: brush each sheet very lightly with a little melted butter; set 1 sheet centrally in the pan, then set 2 sheets in pan so each sheet hangs 4–5 inches over the edge and the rest covers the pan. Then add a central sheet and then 2 more to hang 4–5 inches over the sides. Continue like this until one-third of the sheets are used. Spread large squabs or chicken pieces on the pastry and spoon over 2–3 tablespoons melted butter. Top with 2 sheets of phyllo and spread them with the egg and coriander mixture. Add 2 more sheets of phyllo, sprinkle with almonds mixed with sugar and spoon over 1–2 tablespoons melted butter.

Fold over the hanging sheets of pastry on top to enclose the fillings. Top with the remaining pastry sheets, brushing each one lightly with a little melted butter and overlapping as before but this time tucking the hanging sheets under the pie.

Brush the top with melted butter and bake in a moderate oven (350°F) for 10–15 minutes or until browned.

Place a baking sheet on top, turn pie over and onto baking sheet and remove pan.

Turn oven down to moderately low (325°F) and continue baking for 10–15 minutes or until top is crisp and browned.

Sprinkle with ground cinnamon, cut pie in slices like large bar cookies and serve.

PASTRIES & COOKIES

Baklava
(Greek Honey and Nut Pastries)

1 lb package phyllo pastry
1 cup unsalted butter, melted
1 cup slivered almonds,
    browned and finely chopped
1 cup finely chopped walnuts
1 teaspoon ground cinnamon
30 whole cloves

For syrup
1 cup sugar
1 cup water
1 cup honey
1 tablespoon orange flower
    water

*13 X 9 inch roasting pan or
baking dish*

Makes 20—24 pastries.

Method
Set oven at moderate (350°F) and brush the cake pan with melted butter. Line the pan with half the phyllo sheets, brushing each one with melted butter and pressing it well into the corners and on the sides.

To make the filling: mix the chopped nuts with the cinnamon. Spread the mixture evenly over the pastry and top with the remaining phyllo sheets, brushing each one with butter. Press the sheets firmly together at the edges of the pan or dish and trim with a sharp knife. Brush top with melted butter and score it about ½ inch deep in 2 inch diamonds. Insert a clove in the center of each diamond and bake in heated oven for 30 minutes. Reduce the heat to low (300°F) and continue baking 30 minutes longer or until the top is golden brown.

Meanwhile make the syrup. In a pan heat the sugar with the water until dissolved, add the honey and boil until the syrup spins a thread when a little is lifted on a spoon (234°F on a sugar thermometer). Cool, then stir in the orange flower water and chill until very cold.

As soon as the baklava comes out of the oven, pour over the ice cold syrup, separating the cuts in the pastry with a knife so the syrup runs down between the layers. Let cool, then cut into diamond-shaped pieces for serving.

Koulouria
(Greek Sesame Seed Cookies)

¾ cup unsalted butter
1 cup sugar
2 eggs, beaten to mix
1 teaspoon vanilla
3 cups flour
½ teaspoon salt
1 tablespoon baking powder

For topping
1 egg white, beaten until frothy
2—3 tablespoons sesame seed

Makes 24 cookies.

Method
Cream the butter, beat in the sugar and continue beating until soft and light. Beat in the eggs, a little at a time, and add the vanilla. Sift the flour with the salt and baking powder and stir into the vanilla mixture. Set the oven at moderate (350°F) and grease a baking sheet.

Divide the dough into egg-shaped pieces and roll them on a board with your hands into 6 inch ropes about ½ inch thick. Twist the ropes into coils or figure eights, brush them lightly with beaten egg white and sprinkle tops with sesame seed. Set cookies on the prepared baking sheet and bake in heated oven for 12—15 minutes or until lightly browned.

Transfer to a wire rack to cool.

Eash-el-Asfoor
(Turkish 'Bird's Nests')

½ lb package phyllo pastry
1½ cups shelled pistachios
½ cup sugar
1 cup unsalted butter, melted

To finish
¼ cup honey
juice of ½ lemon

Makes 18—20 pastries.

Method
Blanch the pistachios in boiling water for 1 minute, drain and coarsely chop a third of them. Finely chop the rest and mix with sugar. Set oven at hot (400°F); butter a baking sheet.

Spread a sheet of phyllo on a board or table, brush half the sheet with melted butter and fold it in two and with the other half on top. Place about 2 teaspoons filling along one long edge. Roll up the phyllo around the filling in a cylinder until about two-thirds of the pastry is used. Coil the cylinder round in a spiral and tuck the loose pastry underneath in the center to form a well. Set the pastry on the prepared baking sheet. Shape the remaining sheets of pastry in the same way, using all the filling. Brush each pastry with melted butter and bake in heated oven for 15—20 minutes or until crisp and brown. Take from the oven and fill the hollows with the coarsely chopped pistachios. Melt the honey with the lemon juice and brush over the warm pastries.

Melomacarona
(Greek Spiced Honey Cookies)

4 cups flour
2 teaspoons baking powder
1 cup honey
$\frac{1}{2}$ cup confectioners' sugar
$\frac{1}{2}$ teaspoon ground cinnamon
(optional)
$\frac{1}{2}$ teaspoon ground cloves
(optional)
2 cups olive oil
grated rind and juice 1 orange
2–3 tablespoons finely chopped
walnuts (for sprinkling)

For syrup
1 cup honey
1 cup water

Makes 48–50 cookies.

Method
Sift the flour and baking powder. In a bowl beat the honey with the confectioners' sugar, and the spices, if used, until well blended. Beat the olive oil for several minutes, then gradually beat in the orange juice and rind so the mixture emulsifies. Pour in the honey mixture, still beating constantly. Beat in enough flour to make a smooth paste, then work in the remaining flour with the hand to form a stiff dough.

Set oven at moderate (350°F) and grease a baking sheet. Divide the dough and shape each tablespoon of dough into a small oval, flattening one side slightly. Set ovals on a baking sheet, mark strips like a sun's rays with the back of a knife; sprinkle a few chopped walnuts in the center of each cookie. Bake in heated oven for 13–15 minutes or until light brown.

Bring the honey to a boil with the water, simmer 4–5 minutes, take from the heat and soak the cookies, several at a time, for 2–3 minutes in the hot syrup. Drain them and repeat with remaining cookies, reheating syrup when it cools.

Kaab el Ghzal
(Moroccan Gazelle Horns)

2 cups flour
2 eggs
1 tablespoon orange flower
water
1 tablespoon water

For almond paste
1 cup whole blanched almonds,
ground
1 cup sugar
1 egg white, beaten until frothy
$\frac{1}{4}$ teaspoon almond extract
2 teaspoons orange flower
water (for sprinkling)
1 cup confectioners' sugar
(for rolling)

Makes 16–18 horns.

Method
To make the almond paste: in a mortar and pestle pound almonds with sugar and gradually work in enough egg white and almond extract to form a smooth paste. Alternatively pound the mixture with the end of a rolling pin in a sturdy bowl.

Put the flour in a bowl and add the eggs, orange flower water and water. Work to form a very stiff paste and knead until mixture is smooth. Cover and let stand 15 minutes, then roll out on a lightly floured board as thinly as possible. Cut into 4 inch squares.

Butter a baking sheet and set the oven at moderate (350°F). Divide almond paste into rounds, and roll each into $3\frac{1}{2}$–4 inch cylinders about $\frac{1}{2}$ inch in diameter. Place a cylinder on each square of dough and roll up, sealing ends and edge. Shape cylinders into crescents and set on prepared baking sheet. Bake in heated oven 18–20 minutes or until golden brown.

As soon as horns are cooked, transfer to a rack and sprinkle with orange flower water. Let cool; roll until thickly coated with confectioners' sugar.

Kahve
(Turkish Coffee)

For each person, put a demitasse cup of water in the tanaka (4 cups are the normal maximum) and bring to a boil. Add sugar to taste — a teaspoon per cup gives average sweetness — and top the water with a heaping teaspoon of very finely ground coffee so it floats on the water — the coffee should be ground to a powder. Bring the water again to a boil, take it from the heat and let the froth that has risen die down. Repeat once more, then bring to a boil and stir the coffee well into the water, trying not to lose the froth. Pour at once into demitasse or Turkish coffee cups, shaking the pot slightly as you pour so that a little froth is included in each cup. Serve at once; the grounds will settle at the bottom of the cup and should not be drunk.

Coffee

Coffee was discovered in Arabia about 1,000 years ago and for many years the whole world's supply came from the Yemen in South Arabia.

At first coffee was considered to be an intoxicating drink and therefore forbidden to Muslims by the Koran. But in spite of this it became the great popular drink of the Middle East. The ceremonial serving of coffee to guests expresses the importance of hospitality.

In the Middle East coffee is always freshly made before serving and often the beans are roasted and ground each day. Sugar is always added to the coffee while it cooks, so different brews must be served to please those who like different degrees of sweetness. The special long-handled pot for preparing coffee is called a tanaka.

Turkish coffee is served with an assortment of pastries: eash-el-asfoor (Turkish 'birds' nests'); kaab el ghzal (gazelle horns); diamond-shaped baklava; koulouria (Greek sesame seed cookies); oval melomacarona (Greek spiced honey cookies)

A selection of dried peas and beans includes marrow beans (in basket), split green peas (in wooden bowl), French lentils (in center jar) and red kidney beans (in covered glass jar)

HOW TO COOK DRIED PEAS & BEANS

Both dried peas and beans belong to a large family known as legumes and next to grain, legumes are considered the world's most important food. They are particularly valued in countries where little meat is eaten because of their high protein content.

However, beans play other roles. In Greek and Roman times they were used in elections – a white bean meant 'yes' and a black bean 'no' – so that when Pythagoras, the famous mathematician, told a man to abstain from beans he was urging him to stay out of politics.

Beans have often been used for money because they are easily divided, can be stored without harm and are easy to transport. They only lack the rarity of gold and silver to be the ideal monetary substance.

In medieval Europe, a bean was inserted into the traditional Twelfth Night cake and the man who received the bean became King of the Beans and acted as master of ceremonies for the evening.

Beans became the main ingredient of many American regional dishes as soon as the Indians discovered that beans could be cultivated in poorer soil better than corn and were easy to dry for winter storage.

Dried peas and beans are homey food, generally associated with hearty recipes like split pea soup, baked beans and chili con carne. They are ideally suited to stews and casseroles but they can also be featured more elegantly in salads or as a purée accompaniment to meats.

The range of these legumes is huge, and they all need to be soaked for 8–12 hours before cooking. Presoaked legumes, that save waiting, are available in packages but are more expensive. Check what kind you have and, if presoaked, treat according to package directions.

One cup of dried peas or beans expands after cooking to 2–2½ cups or enough to serve 3–4 people.

KINDS OF DRIED PEAS & BEANS

Chick-peas
Known under several names — Spanish beans, garbanzo beans or ceci peas — chick-peas are delicious combined in a tomato-flavored sauce and spooned over spaghetti and are most popular in the Arab dip called hummus, served with flat bread. Chick-peas are also used in Italian minestrone and in salads. They have irregular shapes, almost like tears, and are firm-textured with a nut-like flavor.

After soaking, simmer $2-2\frac{1}{2}$ hours until tender.

Split Peas
This type of dried pea splits naturally when dried and hulled.

After soaking, simmer $1\frac{1}{2}-2$ hours until tender.

Whole Peas
These come in 2 colors: the yellow variety from field peas and the green ones, dried and hulled, from green peas. They are used mainly in soups flavored with a ham bone. The Germans make yellow peas into a purée and serve it as an accompaniment to sauerkraut.

After soaking, simmer $2\frac{1}{2}-3$ hours until tender.

Black or Turtle Beans
Grown extensively in the South, these beans are used mainly in soups. They are small and oval with black skins and white insides. Black beans are especially popular in South American and Mexican dishes and their flavor blends well with onion, green pepper and ham.

After soaking, simmer beans $2-3$ hours until tender.

Black-eyed Beans
Called black-eyed peas in the South, they are the main ingredients in the hearty Southern dish, Hopping John, where they are mixed with rice, bacon and parsley. Like tiny oval eyes, black-eyed beans are white with a black or yellow spot. After soaking, simmer $1\frac{1}{2}-2$ hours until tender.

Fava or Faba Beans
Known also as broad beans, these are Europe's most important bean. Their flavor is slightly sharp and they are frequently cooked with bacon or ham. Fava beans resemble limas but are rounder.

After soaking, simmer $1-1\frac{1}{2}$ hours until tender.

Pinto Beans
Pale pink and speckled with brown, pinto beans are used interchangeably with **Pink beans**, which are more brownish-red and are sometimes called 'red Mexican' beans. Their flavor blends well with chili powder, tomatoes and onions and both beans are popular in the Southwest.

After soaking, simmer $1\frac{1}{2}-2$ hours until tender.

Red Kidney Beans
These are a reddish-purple color. Next to soybeans they are the most common. They are mellow in flavor and used widely in chili, soups and salads.

After soaking, simmer $1-1\frac{1}{2}$ hours until tender.

Soybeans
The smallest and most important beans, soybeans are used extensively as a source of foods, especially in the Far East because they are high in nutritive value. They are used to make oil and are often a substitute for meat. In cooking they are especially good with tomatoes and cheese and they come in colors ranging from yellow to black.

After soaking, simmer $2\frac{1}{2}-3$ hours until tender.

White Beans
These come in 4 varieties:

Great Northern beans, grown in the Midwest, are one of the most common beans used for baking because of their mellow flavor.

After soaking, simmer $2-3$ hours until tender.

Marrow Beans are used for baked beans and in soups and stews. Their flavor blends well with brown sugar, molasses and salt pork. They are the largest and roundest of the white beans and are grown mainly in the East.

After soaking, simmer $2-2\frac{1}{2}$ hours until tender.

Navy Beans were named by the men of the U.S. Navy who were served them too often. Grown mainly in Michigan, they are smaller than Great Northern beans and a little tough. They are usually the beans used in canned pork and beans.

After soaking, simmer 3 hours until tender.

Pea Beans are the smallest white beans and are used for Boston baked beans.

After soaking, simmer about 3 hours until tender.

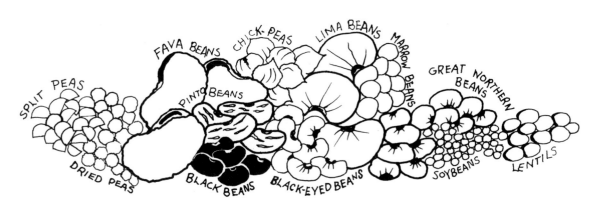

Lentils

These come in 2 varieties: the French lentil, gray in color, and the Egyptian red-orange lentil. They are delicious puréed and served hot as an accompaniment to roasts and chops and are excellent in stews and casseroles and in salads.

After soaking, simmer 1–1½ hours until tender.

Lima Beans

Generally pale green, limas are a flat kidney-shaped bean available in a variety of sizes and grown extensively in California. In the South, they come speckled with purple and are called calico or speckled butter beans. They are used in stews or puréed and served with lamb.

After soaking, simmer about 30–45 minutes until tender. Dried limas, strangely enough, take about the same time to cook as fresh lima beans.

To Soak and Cook Dried Peas and Beans

1 Wash legumes unless the package states otherwise and pick over to remove any grit.
2 Soak legumes, if necessary, in 3–4 times their volume of lukewarm water for 8 hours or overnight. Discard any that float. If they must be left longer, change the water or they may start to ferment. They can be tenderized quickly by covering with cold water, bringing to a boil and simmering 2 minutes but this method is not so thorough as long soaking.
3 Drain legumes, cover with fresh warm water, add a lid and simmer until tender. Do not add salt until halfway through cooking to avoid toughening the outer skins. Cooking time depends on the age and on the type of legumes; for example, limas take about 45 minutes, lentils take about 1½ hours and navy beans, the toughest of all, need up to 3 hours. For some recipes the legumes should only be simmered in water for a short time and cooking is completed in some other way. For specific **cooking times**, see under individual names on opposite page.
4 The simplest way to test if done is to lift out a few beans on a spoon; taste one, or if they burst when you blow on them, they are done.

Boula Boula

½ cup (¼ lb) split green peas, cooked and drained
4 cups canned green turtle soup
¼ cup Madeira or sherry
salt and pepper
½ cup heavy cream, stiffly whipped (for topping)

Method

Work the cooked split peas through a sieve or purée in a blender with a little of the turtle soup, then stir remaining soup into pea purée. Simmer 20 minutes, add Madeira or sherry and seasoning and reheat without boiling. Pour soup into heatproof bowls and top each with 2 tablespoons whipped cream. Broil soup for 1 minute under the broiler or until lightly browned and serve at once.

Black Bean Soup

1 cup (½ lb) dried black or turtle beans, soaked
1 quart water
ham bone
2 stalks of celery, chopped
1 medium onion, sliced
bouquet garni
salt and pepper
3 tablespoons Madeira or juice of ½ lemon
1 hard-cooked egg, chopped (for garnish)

Method

Drain the beans and put in a kettle with the water, ham bone, celery, onion, bouquet garni and pepper to taste. Cover, bring to a boil and simmer 3 hours or until beans are very tender. Discard the bone and bouquet garni and work bean mixture through a sieve or a food mill or purée in a blender. Return bean purée to the kettle, add a little more water if the soup is very thick and bring to a boil. Add Madeira, or lemon juice, taste for seasoning and serve with a little chopped hard-cooked egg sprinkled over the soup.

Lentil Soup

1 cup (½ lb) dried Egyptian or French lentils, soaked
1 onion, chopped
6 cups cold water
salt and pepper
ham bone
½–1 cup stock (optional)

For liaison (optional)
1 egg yolk
3 tablespoons heavy cream

For garnish
1 tablespoon chopped fresh mint
2 slices of bacon, diced and crisply fried
2–3 slices of bread, crusts removed, cut in cubes and fried in 3–4 tablespoons oil and butter, mixed (for croûtons) – optional

Method

Drain lentils and put in a kettle with the onion, water, a little pepper and ham bone. Cover, bring to a boil and simmer 1½ hours or until lentils are very soft. Drain lentils, reserving liquid, and discard ham bone. Work lentils and onion through a sieve or food mill or purée in a blender with a little of the liquid.

Rinse out pan, return purée to it and gradually stir in reserved liquid. If soup is very thick, add a little stock.

Reheat the soup, and taste for seasoning. If adding liaison to enrich it, mix egg yolk and cream in a bowl, stir in a little of the hot soup and add this to remaining soup in pan. Reheat until it thickens slightly but do not let it boil.

Serve soup in bowls, sprinkled with a little chopped mint and crisp bacon and serve croûtons separately, if you like.

Bean and leek soup, eaten with bread, is a meal in itself

Bean and Leek Soup

1 cup (½ lb) pea beans, soaked overnight and drained
¼ lb piece of bacon, diced
4 carrots, diced
5–6 medium leeks, diced
bouquet garni
1 clove of garlic, crushed
salt and pepper
8 cups stock
small head of green cabbage, shredded

Like garbure paysanne, this soup is often eaten with bread as a meal in itself. It serves 6–8 people.

Method

Simmer the beans, covered, in half the stock for 2 hours. If all the stock is absorbed during cooking, add water so the pan is not dry.

In a kettle fry the bacon until it is beginning to brown. Add the carrots and leeks, cover and cook slowly for 5–7 minutes or until the fat is absorbed.

Add the beans and their cooking liquid, the bouquet garni, garlic, seasoning and remaining stock, cover and simmer ¾ hour or until the beans are tender. Add the cabbage and simmer 15 minutes longer.

Taste the soup for seasoning and serve with French bread.

A warming green pea soup is an ideal appetizer for cold days. Pile a few croûtons in the center of each bowl before serving

Green Pea Soup

1 cup (½ lb) split green peas, soaked
salt and pepper
3 tablespoons butter
1 medium onion, thinly sliced
1 medium carrot, thinly sliced
1 clove of garlic, crushed
ham bone with a little meat on it and 3 cups water, or 6–7 cups beef stock
1 teaspoon sugar
2–3 sprigs of fresh mint or 1 teaspoon dried mint
croûtons (for serving)

Method

Drain peas, put in a pan with warm water to cover, and add lid. Bring to a boil and simmer 1 hour.

Melt 2 tablespoons butter in a kettle, add onion, carrot, and garlic, cover and cook over low heat for 5 minutes. Add peas with their liquid and the ham bone with water or the stock. Add pepper and sugar, cover and simmer 1 hour or until all vegetables are tender. If soup gets very thick, add more stock or water.

Discard ham bone after reserving any meat. Work through a sieve or food mill or purée soup in a blender.

Rinse out kettle, return soup to it, add mint and bring to a boil, whisking well. Thin soup, if necessary, with more stock or water, taste for seasoning and simmer 3–5 minutes. Chop meat from ham bone and add to soup.

Just before serving, discard fresh mint and beat remaining butter into soup. Pile a few croûtons in center of each bowl.

Fava bean soup, made with salt pork, cabbage and spices, is sprinkled with parsley for serving

Fava Bean Soup

2 cups (10–12 oz) dried fava
   beans, soaked overnight
   and drained
1–2 tablespoons oil
$\frac{1}{4}$ lb piece of salt pork,
   blanched, drained and diced
1 onion, chopped
3 tomatoes, peeled, seeded
   and chopped or 2 cups
   canned tomatoes, crushed
$\frac{1}{2}$ teaspoon paprika
bouquet garni (3 whole cloves,
   and 6 allspice berries, tied
   in a cheesecloth bag)
2 quarts water
salt and pepper
1 small cabbage, shredded
2 tablespoons chopped parsley
   (for sprinkling)

Method

In a kettle heat the oil and fry the salt pork until browned. Add the onion and cook over low heat until soft but not browned. Add the drained beans, tomatoes, paprika, bag of spices and water and cover. Bring to a boil and simmer 1–1$\frac{1}{4}$ hours or until the beans are almost tender. Season to taste half way through cooking and remove cheesecloth bag if the soup is already spicy enough.

   Add shredded cabbage and cook 20–25 minutes longer or until the cabbage and beans are tender. Discard cheesecloth bag, if not already done, taste the soup for seasoning and sprinkle each bowl with chopped parsley before serving.

Puchero

1 cup ($\frac{1}{2}$ lb) red or brown
   kidney beans, soaked
1$\frac{1}{2}$ lb smoked pork chops, or
   1 lb brisket of beef, cut in
   1$\frac{1}{2}$ inch cubes
2 tablespoons oil
1 large onion, sliced
1 large carrot, sliced
1–2 cloves of garlic, crushed
2 teaspoons tomato paste
1$\frac{1}{2}$–2 cups stock or water
salt and pepper
bouquet garni
$\frac{1}{2}$ lb Chorizo sausage
2 tomatoes, peeled, seeded and
   quartered
2 slices of canned pimiento,
   drained and cut in strips

Puchero (a stew) is of Spanish origin and there are several versions; this particular recipe comes from South America.

Method

Drain beans, put in a kettle, cover with cold water and add the lid. Bring to a boil and simmer 1$\frac{1}{2}$ hours. Put smoked pork or beef in separate pan of cold water, bring to a boil and cook 1 hour. Drain both beans and meat.

   In a large kettle or flameproof casserole heat the oil, add onion, carrot and garlic and cook 4–5 minutes until soft. Add beans, tomato paste and 1$\frac{1}{2}$ cups stock or water with a little salt and pepper and the bouquet garni. Bring to a boil, add pork or beef, cover and simmer 1 hour. Blanch the sausage, drain and add to the pot. Simmer 30 minutes longer. If the bean mixture becomes dry during cooking, add more stock.

   When meat and beans are tender, add tomatoes and pimiento, cover and cook 5–10 minutes longer. The puchero should be rich and thick.

   Take out the sausages and

slice them. Return to the pan and taste the dish for seasoning. Remove bouquet garni before serving.

Chicken with Chick-peas

3$\frac{1}{2}$–4 lb roasting chicken
1 cup ($\frac{1}{2}$ lb) chick-peas, soaked
1 onion, finely chopped
2 tablespoons oil
1 teaspoon turmeric
1 teaspoon ground coriander
juice of 1 lemon
2 cloves of garlic, crushed
salt
black pepper, freshly ground

Method

Drain chick-peas.

   In a deep flameproof casserole fry the onion in the oil until soft. Stir in turmeric and coriander, add chicken and cook until a deep golden brown on all sides. Add the chick-peas with 2 cups of water, lemon juice, garlic and pepper.

   Cover, bring to a boil and simmer on top of the stove or bake in a moderate oven (350°F) for 1–1$\frac{1}{4}$ hours or until the chicken is very tender, adding more liquid if the chick-peas look dry during cooking. When done, the chick-peas should be very soft and moist without being wet.

   Serve chicken whole in the casserole surrounded by chick-peas.

Cooking times for the different kinds of dried peas and beans can be found under the individual names of legumes on pages 100–101.

Navy Beans with Sausages

1 cup ($\frac{1}{2}$ lb) dried navy beans, cooked and drained
1 lb pork sausages
2 tablespoons butter
1 medium onion, finely chopped
2 teaspoons flour
2 tablespoons stock
$\frac{1}{2}$ cup white wine
squeeze of lemon juice
1 tablespoon butter
salt and pepper

Method
In a skillet fry the sausages until brown on all sides, pricking them to release the fat. Discard all but 2–3 tablespoons fat. Add cooked beans and cook over brisk heat until they are lightly browned and have absorbed all the fat from the sausages. Transfer to a serving dish and keep hot.

Wipe out the skillet, heat the butter and brown the onion; stir in the flour, pour in stock and wine and bring to a boil, stirring. Simmer 10 minutes, add the lemon juice and pour over the beans and sausages. Dot with butter and shake well until mixed. Season and serve very hot.

Cooking times for the different kinds of dried peas and beans can be found under the individual names of legumes on pages 100–101.

Cassoulet

4$\frac{1}{2}$ cups (2 lb) dried white Great Northern beans, cooked and drained
$\frac{1}{2}$ lb lean salt pork
4 cloves of garlic, finely chopped
3–4 lb duck
$\frac{1}{4}$ cup butter, or bacon drippings
1 lb boned shoulder of lamb, cut in cubes
1 lb boneless loin of pork, cut in cubes
bouquet garni
salt
black pepper, freshly ground
$\frac{1}{2}$ lb garlic sausage
3 medium tomatoes, peeled, seeded and chopped, or 2 cups (1 lb) canned tomatoes
1 tablespoon tomato paste
1 teaspoon sugar
$\frac{1}{4}$ cup browned breadcrumbs

This dish from the Languedoc region of France contains many of the specialties of that area. This recipe is simplified, with duck replacing the traditional pickled goose. Garlic sausage is available at delicatessens. Serves 6–8 people.

Method
Put drained beans in a large flameproof casserole with the salt pork and garlic. Add water to cover, put on the lid and simmer gently for 1 hour. Drain beans and salt pork, reserving the cooking liquid.

Cut duck in 4 pieces, discarding the backbone. In the casserole, heat butter or drippings and brown the duck on all sides. Take out, add the lamb and brown also. Take out and brown the loin of pork. Add the beans and salt pork, put back the duck and lamb and stir once or twice to mix. Add the bouquet garni with a little salt and plenty of pepper.

Moisten with some of the reserved bean liquid, cover and simmer very slowly on top of the stove or in a low oven (300°F) for 2$\frac{1}{2}$ hours, adding more cooking liquid from time to time, if necessary. Add the garlic sausage and continue cooking 1–1$\frac{1}{2}$ hours or until the beans are very tender. Take out the salt pork and sausage, slice them and replace in the casserole.

In a skillet simmer tomatoes until pulpy, add tomato paste, sugar and seasoning. Spoon this mixture over the cassoulet, shake gently to mix, then sprinkle with the browned breadcrumbs. Bake in a moderately hot oven (375°F) for $\frac{3}{4}$–1 hour longer or until brown.

Chili Con Carne

1 cup ($\frac{1}{2}$ lb) dried red kidney beans, cooked and drained
1$\frac{1}{2}$ lb ground beef
2 tablespoons oil, or bacon drippings
2 onions, finely chopped
2 tablespoons chili powder
2 tablespoons ground cumin
2 teaspoons paprika
about 1$\frac{1}{2}$ cups canned tomatoes
salt and pepper

Method
In a skillet heat the oil or drippings and fry onion until soft. Stir in the chili powder, cumin and paprika and add the ground beef. Cook over medium heat, stirring to separate the meat until it browns, then add the drained beans and the tomatoes. Season, cover and simmer 1–1$\frac{1}{2}$ hours or until the mixture is thick and the beans are very tender. Add a little water if the chili looks too thick during cooking. Serve with crusty bread and beer.

Boston Baked Beans

2$\frac{1}{2}$ cups (1 lb) dried pea beans, soaked and cooked
$\frac{1}{4}$ lb lean salt pork
1 onion, quartered
1 teaspoon salt
$\frac{1}{2}$ cup molasses
$\frac{1}{2}$ teaspoon dry mustard
1 tablespoon brown sugar

Method
Blanch the salt pork, drain it and score the top with 1 inch deep cuts, $\frac{1}{2}$ inch apart, or cut into chunks.

Drain the cooked beans, reserving the cooking liquid, and put them in a bean pot or casserole. Bury the onion and pork (if using in one piece) in the beans, so the scored surface of the pork is exposed. Mix the salt, molasses, mustard and brown sugar with 1 cup of the reserved cooking liquid and pour it over the beans. Cover and bake in a low oven (300°F) for 6–8 hours, adding more reserved liquid as needed to prevent the beans from becoming dry.

Uncover the pot for the last hour of baking so the pork becomes brown and crisp.

Boston baked beans — dried pea beans are baked with chunks of salt pork

Fava beans ménagère are served in a creamy sauce and garnished with tomato

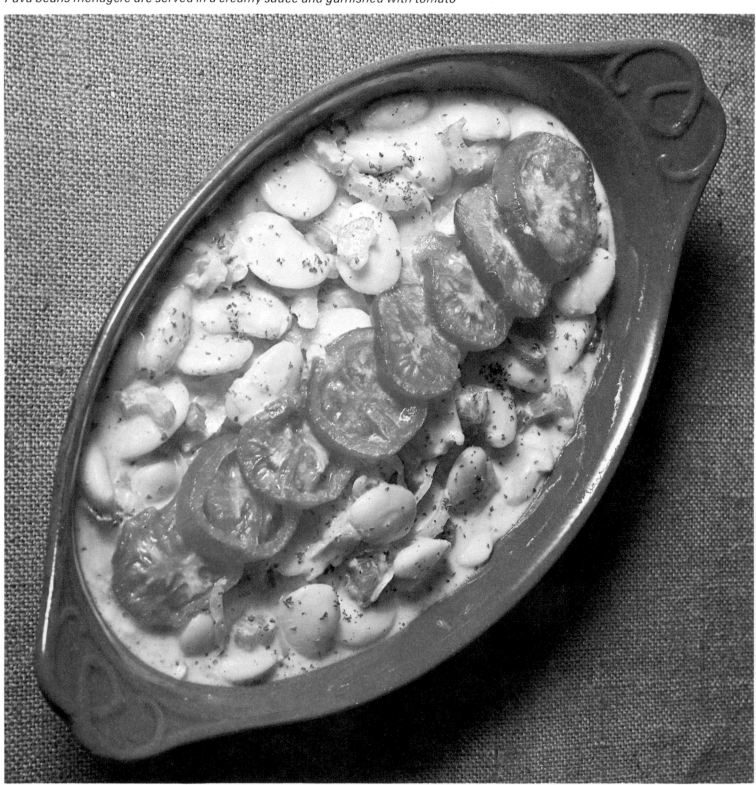

Add fava beans, celery and onion to the white sauce

Arrange broiled tomato slices on fava beans and serve

Cooking times for the different kinds of dried peas and beans can be found under the individual names of legumes on pages 100–101.

Fava Beans Ménagère

1 cup ($\frac{1}{2}$ lb) fava beans, soaked
2 stalks of celery, sliced
1 onion, sliced
1 bay leaf
salt and pepper
thick white sauce (made with
   3 tablespoons butter,
   2 tablespoons flour,
   1 cup milk)
1 tablespoon chopped parsley
2 tablespoons heavy cream
2 tomatoes, peeled and sliced
1 tablespoon sugar
$\frac{1}{2}$ tablespoon butter

Serve with roast lamb or beef.

Method
Drain the beans and put in a pan with celery, onion and bay leaf; cover with boiling water, season, add the lid and simmer 1–1$\frac{1}{2}$ hours or until tender.

Drain bean mixture, reserving 1 cup cooking liquid, and discard bay leaf. Add bean mixture to white sauce, shake pan gently to mix well, then add parsley, cream and reserved cooking liquid. Taste for seasoning and transfer to a serving dish and keep warm.

Sprinkle tomato slices with salt, pepper and sugar, dot with butter and broil 1–2 minutes until lightly cooked. Arrange them on the beans and serve.

Black or Lima Bean Purée

1 cup ($\frac{1}{2}$ lb) black or turtle
   beans, or lima beans, soaked
   and cooked
$\frac{1}{4}$ cup oil
1 yellow onion, chopped
2 cloves of garlic, crushed
1 tablespoon wine vinegar
$\frac{1}{4}$ cup sour cream
salt
black pepper, freshly ground
1 red or Bermuda onion, very
   finely chopped (optional)

Serve with roast lamb or baked ham.

Method
Drain beans, reserving liquid.

In a skillet heat the oil and fry yellow onion with garlic until soft. Add to the beans and work through a sieve or food mill or purée mixture in blender with a little of the cooking liquid.

Return bean purée to the pan with the vinegar and sour cream and seasoning to taste. Reheat thoroughly but do not overcook or sour cream will curdle. Stir in the chopped red or Bermuda onion, if used, and serve hot.

Lentil Purée

1 cup lentils
1 onion, stuck with 1 clove
1 carrot, cut in rounds
bouquet garni
salt and pepper
little stock (optional)
$\frac{1}{4}$ cup butter
1 stalk of celery, very finely
   chopped

This is an excellent accompaniment to casseroled pork or veal. Dried peas may be used instead of lentils.

Method
Soak the lentils according to package directions. Drain and combine in a saucepan with onion, carrot, bouquet garni, a little salt and plenty of water. Simmer for 1$\frac{1}{2}$ hours or until tender.

Remove bouquet garni and take clove out of onion; work mixture through a sieve or purée in a blender. Reheat and thin with a little stock if purée is too thick. Take from the heat and beat in the butter with pepper to taste. Before serving, stir in chopped celery.

Beans Maître d'Hôtel

1 cup ($\frac{1}{2}$ lb) dried fava or lima
   beans, soaked
$\frac{1}{4}$ lb salt pork
1 onion, stuck with 1 clove
bouquet garni
3 tablespoons butter
1 clove of garlic, crushed
1 tablespoon chopped parsley
juice of $\frac{1}{2}$ lemon
black pepper, freshly ground
salt

Serve with steak or veal.

Method
Drain the beans and put them in a pan with water to cover, add the salt pork, onion and bouquet garni and simmer 1–1$\frac{1}{2}$ hours for fava beans or 30–45 minutes for limas or until beans are tender. Drain beans, reserving $\frac{3}{4}$ cup of their cooking liquid, and discard onion and bouquet garni. Cut salt pork into strips. Return beans and salt pork to the pan with the reserved liquid and heat gently. Cream butter and stir in the garlic, parsley, lemon juice and pepper. Drop it into the pan in pieces. Cover, turn off the heat and shake the pan gently until butter is mixed with beans. Taste for seasoning and serve.

Kidney Bean Purée

1 cup ($\frac{1}{2}$ lb) red kidney beans,
   soaked and cooked
2 tablespoons butter
$\frac{1}{2}$ teaspoon allspice
$\frac{1}{4}$ teaspoon ground nutmeg
$\frac{1}{4}$ teaspoon ground coriander
$\frac{1}{2}$ teaspoon chili powder
salt and pepper

Serve with roast or sautéed
pork.

Method
Drain the beans, reserving the
liquid, and work through a
sieve or food mill or purée
them in a blender with a little
cooking liquid.

Melt the butter, add bean
purée with the spices and
seasoning to taste and cook,
stirring, until very hot, adding
a little cooking liquid, if
necessary, to make a smooth
purée that falls fairly easily
from a spoon.

Chick-pea Salad

1 cup chick-peas, cooked and
   drained
1 canned or fresh green chili
   pepper, seeded and chopped
1 slice of canned pimiento,
   drained and chopped
1 cup chopped celery
2 tablespoons drained capers
5–6 scallions, trimmed and
   chopped
$\frac{1}{4}$ cup olive oil
$1\frac{1}{2}$ tablespoons lemon juice
salt
black pepper, freshly ground
few lettuce leaves (for serving)

Serve with roast pork.

Method
Add chili, pimiento, celery,
capers and scallions to
drained chick-peas. Mix oil
and lemon juice with salt and

a little pepper, spoon over
chick-pea mixture and taste
for seasoning.

Arrange the lettuce leaves
around a salad bowl and pile
the chick-pea salad in the
center.

Tomato, Anchovy and Bean Salad

2 tomatoes, peeled, seeded and
   cut in strips
12 anchovy fillets, soaked in a
   little milk
1 cup ($\frac{1}{2}$ lb) dried Navy or pea
   beans, cooked
1 shallot, finely chopped
2 tablespoons heavy cream
vinaigrette dressing (made with
   $\frac{1}{4}$ cup red wine vinegar,
   6 tablespoons oil, salt,
   pepper and little sugar)
1 tablespoon chopped chives

This salad is a good accompaniment for cold roast lamb.

Method
Cool beans in their cooking
liquid and drain them. Drain
the anchovies and cut in
$\frac{1}{2}$ inch strips. Whisk shallot
and cream into vinaigrette
dressing and stir in tomatoes
and anchovies. Spoon dressing over beans, sprinkle with
chopped chives and serve.

Lentil Salad

1 cup ($\frac{1}{2}$ lb) dried Egyptian or
   French lentils, soaked and
   cooked with a bouquet garni
$\frac{1}{2}$ cup vinaigrette dressing
1 clove of garlic, crushed
salt
black pepper, freshly ground
8–10 small onions, sliced
2 tomatoes, peeled, seeded
   and coarsely chopped

For garnish
small bunch of celery
1 lemon, cut in wedges

Serve as a cocktail hors
d'œuvre or appetizer with hot
Arab bread (pita) or crackers.

Method
Drain the lentils, reserving the
cooking liquid, and discard
bouquet garni. Work them
through a sieve or food mill or
purée in a blender with a little
of the cooking liquid; stir in a
little more cooking liquid to
form a purée that falls fairly
easily from a spoon. Cool.

To prepare garnish: wash
the celery, cut in fine, 2 inch
strips, lengthwise, and soak in
ice water for 1 hour or until
they curl.

Stir vinaigrette dressing,
garlic and plenty of seasoning
into the lentil purée. Mix in
sliced onions and tomatoes
and pile into a serving dish.
Surround with celery curls and
lemon wedges.

Marrow Beans in Cream Sauce

1 cup ($\frac{1}{2}$ lb) dried marrow
   beans, soaked overnight
   and drained
1 onion, stuck with 1 clove
bouquet garni
salt and pepper
$\frac{1}{4}$ cup butter
1 onion, chopped
1 clove of garlic, crushed
3 tablespoons flour
$1\frac{1}{2}$ cups heavy cream

Serve with baked ham or roast
lamb.

Method
Put the drained beans in a
pan with the whole onion,
bouquet garni and water to
cover. Simmer 2–$2\frac{1}{2}$ hours or
until the beans are tender,
adding salt half way through
cooking. Drain the beans.

In a saucepan melt the
butter, add the chopped onion
and garlic and sauté until the
onion is soft but not browned.
Stir in the flour, pour in the
cream and bring to a boil,
stirring constantly. Simmer 2
minutes, add the beans and
season well. Heat the beans
thoroughly and serve.

Cooking times for the
different kinds of dried
peas and beans can be
found under the individual
names of legumes on
pages 100–101.

Marrow beans in cream sauce are a good accompaniment to baked or roast meat

Scallops Dugléré are browned before serving (recipe is on page 114)

A LUXURY MENU

Coquilles St. Jacques Duglére
or
Iced Curry Soup

Braised Fillet of Beef Chasseur
Fondant Potatoes or Buttered Noodles

Boîte au Chocolat aux Fruits
(Chocolate Box with Fruit)

White wine – Sauternes (Bordeaux)
or Sauvignon Blanc (California)

Red wine – Morey St. Denis (Burgundy)
or Pinot Noir (California)

For this menu, you have a choice of appetizer – scallops, cooked in classic style with tomatoes, parsley and white wine, or an iced curry soup. The entrée, also a classic, is fillet of beef chasseur, braised with wine and mushrooms. Dessert for the dinner menu is a chocolate cake with a difference – liqueur-soaked sponge cake topped with cream and fruit and surrounded by wafer-thin chocolate squares.

As an unusual idea begin with a sweet white wine to go with the special cream sauce for the scallops. The Sauternes of Bordeaux are glorious and California affords a counterpart in a sweet Sauvignon Blanc. Such lush wines are best served cold – one glass per guest should be enough. The choice for the beef can be more traditional but no less grand – a major Burgundy like Morey St. Denis is ideal. A less fullsome, native wine is a Pinot Noir from the San Francisco Bay area.

113

TIMETABLE

Day before
Make Espagnole sauce for beef fillet.

Bake sponge cake and keep in airtight container. Make chocolate squares; store in cool place.
Make stock for soup.

Morning
Poach scallops, make and pour over sauce. Prepare mashed potatoes and pipe around scallops; add butter and breadcrumbs ready for reheating. Cover and keep in cool place.
Make curry soup, cool, cover and chill; make curry base for cream topping.
Trim mushrooms for beef and leave whole. Tie beef (if necessary).
Prepare vegetables.

Assemble ingredients for final cooking from 7 p.m. for dinner around 8 p.m.

You will find that **cooking times** given in the individual recipes for these dishes have sometimes been adapted in the timetable to help you when cooking and serving this menu as a party meal.

Order of Work

7:00
Set oven at moderate (350°F). Whip cream for cake *and for curry soup.*
Toss fruit for cake with sugar, complete cake and chill.
Complete curry cream topping.
7:15
Start browning beef.
7:30
Put beef in oven. Start cooking fondant potatoes *or simmer noodles.* Cook green vegetable.
7:40
Reheat scallops in oven with beef.
7:45
Sauté mushrooms and shallot for beef; reduce wine and add tomato paste.
Drain noodles, cover with warm water and keep warm.
Transfer vegetables and potatoes to serving dish and keep warm.
7:55
Transfer beef to platter and keep warm.
Strain sauce, add to mushroom mixture and keep warm.
8:00
Serve appetizer.
Just before serving, carve beef, arrange on platter with mushrooms; spoon some sauce over meat slices.
Drain noodles and toss with butter just before serving.

Appetizer

Coquilles St. Jacques Duglére
(Scallops Duglére)

1 lb sea scallops
1 shallot or small onion, sliced
salt
6 peppercorns
$\frac{1}{2}$ bay leaf
$\frac{1}{2}$ cup water
squeeze of lemon juice
2 tablespoons browned breadcrumbs (to finish)
2 tablespoons butter (to finish)

For cream sauce
$\frac{3}{4}$ cup light cream
2 tablespoons butter
$1\frac{1}{2}$ tablespoons flour
2 tomatoes, peeled, seeded and cut in strips
2 teaspoons chopped parsley

For mashed potatoes
3 medium potatoes
1 tablespoon butter
$\frac{1}{4}$ cup hot milk
pepper

4 scallop shells or individual ramekins; pastry bag and large star tube

Method
To make mashed potatoes: cook potatoes in boiling salted water for 15–20 minutes until tender. Drain them, dry a few moments over low heat, then mash and beat to a purée or work through a sieve. Beat in the butter, salt and pepper, pour over the milk, cover and reserve.

Put scallops in a pan with shallot or onion, salt, peppercorns, bay leaf, water and lemon juice. Cover and poach very gently for 6–7 minutes or until scallops are just cooked and have no transparent center when sliced. Strain scallops and reserve cooking liquid.

Watchpoint: do not let scallops boil as this makes them tough.

To make cream sauce: melt butter in a saucepan, remove from the heat and stir in the flour. Blend in reserved liquid from scallops, bring to a boil, stirring constantly, until sauce thickens. Simmer 2–3 minutes, pour in cream and bring just to a boil. Taste for seasoning, then add tomatoes and chopped parsley.

Slice or quarter scallops, put them in the buttered scallop shells or ramekins and spoon over sauce. Beat mashed potatoes to mix, put into pastry bag fitted with the star tube and pipe a border around the edge of each shell or ramekin; sprinkle the centers lightly with browned breadcrumbs and dot with remaining butter.

If scallops are prepared ahead of time, before serving reheat them in a hot oven (400°F) for 10–15 minutes until very hot and browned. If they are cooked just before serving and the scallops, sauce and potatoes are hot, put under broiler for a few moments to glaze and brown potatoes.

Ramekins are small heatproof dishes shaped like miniature soufflé dishes.

Iced curry soup is topped with cream flavored with port, curry powder and apricot

Iced Curry Soup

1 tablespoon curry powder
   (or to taste)
2 tablespoons butter
4 shallots or 1 medium onion,
   finely chopped
2 tablespoons flour
4 cups chicken or well-flavored
   vegetable stock
strip of lemon rind
bay leaf
$\frac{3}{4}$ cup boiling water
1 tablespoon blanched, ground
   almonds
1 tablespoons unsweetened
   flaked coconut
2 teaspoons arrowroot (mixed
   to a paste with 2 tablespoons
   cold stock or water)
salt and pepper (optional)

To finish
$\frac{1}{4}$ cup port
1 teaspoon curry powder
2 teaspoons apricot jam
$\frac{1}{4}$ cup heavy cream, whipped
   until it holds a soft shape

Method

In a pan melt about three-quarters of the butter add shallot or onion and cook slowly until golden brown. Stir in curry powder and flour and continue cooking gently, stirring frequently, for 2–3 minutes. Stir in remaining butter, pour in stock and bring to a boil. Add lemon rind and bay leaf and simmer soup for 20 minutes. Strain, return soup to the pan and simmer 10–15 minutes longer.

Pour the boiling water over the almonds and coconut and let stand 30 minutes; squeeze mixture in a piece of cheesecloth and add this liquid to soup. Add arrowroot paste and cook, stirring constantly, until it just comes to a boil and thickens. Taste for seasoning, strain soup again and cool before chilling.

To finish: in a pan mix port and curry powder together and simmer until reduced by half. Cool, then mix with apricot jam or purée and squeeze mixture in a piece of cheesecloth to extract the liquid; stir this into the whipped cream.

Serve chilled curry soup in individual bowls with a spoonful of flavored cream on top.

115

Braised Fillet of Beef Chasseur

2–2½ lb fillet of beef
1 tablespoon oil
1 large onion, sliced
2 large carrots, sliced
2 cups (½ lb) mushrooms
1 tablespoon butter
1 shallot, finely chopped
½ cup white wine
1 teaspoon tomato paste

For Espagnole sauce
3 tablespoons oil
2 tablespoons finely diced onion
2 tablespoons finely diced carrot
1 tablespoon finely diced celery
1½ tablespoons flour
2 teaspoons tomato paste
1 tablespoon chopped mushrooms
2½ cups well-flavored brown stock
bouquet garni
salt and pepper

Method

First prepare Espagnole sauce. This may be done the day before if more convenient.

Set oven at moderate (350°F).

If butcher has not already done so, tie beef with string at 2 inch intervals to keep it in shape during browning. Heat oil in a heavy flameproof casserole, put in beef and brown on all sides. Remove from the pot, reduce heat and add onion and carrot. Cover pot and cook gently for about 10 minutes or until vegetables absorb the oil and begin to brown. Return beef to the pot and pour over Espagnole sauce. Cover with foil and a tight-fitting lid and bring to a boil. Braise in heated oven for 25–35 minutes for rare beef.

Trim mushroom stems level with the caps and sauté caps quickly in the butter until tender. Stir in shallot and cook for about 1 minute, then pour in wine and continue cooking until reduced by half. Stir in tomato paste. Remove beef from pot and keep warm. Strain sauce onto mushroom mixture, bring just to a boil and taste for seasoning.

Carve beef in ½ inch slices, discarding strings, and arrange down the center of a hot platter. Lift mushrooms from sauce with a slotted spoon and arrange them at each side of the beef. Moisten beef with 2–3 tablespoons sauce and serve the rest separately. Serve with fondant potatoes (see page 80) and a green vegetable of your choice.

Note: if you are serving the scallops and want to avoid having potatoes twice, serve the beef with buttered noodles.

After skimming twice, strain Espagnole sauce

Buttered Belgian Endive

8 heads of Belgian endive
2 tablespoons butter
salt and pepper
juice of ½ lemon
2 tablespoons water
1 tablespoon finely chopped parsley (for garnish)

Method

Rub the butter over the bottom of a shallow flame-proof casserole or skillet. Trim off the bottoms and any damaged outer leaves of the endive and cut the heads into diagonal slices about 1 inch thick. Put them in the pan with salt and pepper to taste, lemon juice and water.

Press a piece of buttered foil on top of the endive and cover with a lid. Cook over low heat for 7–8 minutes or until the endive is tender, shaking the pan occasionally. Sprinkle with chopped parsley and serve.

Buttered Noodles

½ lb package of noodles
2 tablespoons butter
salt
black pepper, freshly ground

Method

Cook noodles in plenty of boiling salted water, 2–3 quarts at least, for 8–10 minutes or until the noodles are tender but still firm (al dente). Stir gently from time to time to prevent noodles from sticking to bottom of pan. When cooked, they should look creamy and opaque and can be severed with a thumbnail (or taste one to see if done).

Watchpoint: do not overcook noodles because they become sticky and pasty.

Pour at once into a colander, rinse in hot water and drain well. Rinse pan used to cook noodles and add the butter. Return noodles to the pan and toss over low heat for 1–2 minutes. Season with salt and black pepper.

Note: if the noodles must be kept hot before serving, pour about 1 cup hot water into the pan, put in drained noodles, cover and keep warm at the side of the stove. When ready to serve, drain off the water, add butter and seasonings and toss the noodles.

Braised beef chasseur is moistened with a brown sauce flavored with tomato and white wine, and garnished with mushrooms

For chocolate squares: when chocolate is hard, remove the squares from wax paper with a small metal spatula

Spoon raspberries, sweetened with sugar, on top of cake before adding remaining cream

Boîte au Chocolat aux Fruits
(Chocolate Box with Fruit)

For sponge cake
¾ cup flour
pinch of salt
3 eggs, separated
½ cup sugar
1 tablespoon boiling water

To finish
3 squares (3 oz) semisweet chocolate, chopped in coarse pieces
2–3 tablespoons rum, kirsch or Grand Marnier
1 pint fresh raspberries or strawberries, or 2–3 fresh peaches
sugar (to taste – to sweeten fruit)
1 cup heavy cream, stiffly whipped

8 inch square cake pan; 8 inch square of wax paper

Another version of boîte au chocolat, using chestnuts, was given in Volume 10.

Method
Set oven at moderate (350°F). Grease and flour the cake pan.

To make sponge cake: sift flour with salt. Beat egg yolks with half the sugar and the boiling water in a bowl over a pan of hot water until mixture is thick and leaves a ribbon trail on itself when the beater is lifted; take from heat and continue beating until cool. If using an electric beater, no heat is necessary.

Beat egg whites until they hold a stiff peak, then beat in the remaining sugar until mixture is glossy. Cut and fold this into the yolk mixture alternately with the flour. Spoon batter into prepared pan and bake in the heated oven for about 25 minutes or until cake begins to shrink from the sides of the pan. Turn out onto a wire rack and cool.

Melt chocolate on a heat-proof plate over a pan of hot water; do not heat above lukewarm. Spread evenly and thinly (about one-eighth inch thick) over the wax paper. When firm, using a sharp knife mark into small squares about 1¾ inches or slightly larger than the depth of the sponge cake. Chill on the paper in refrigerator until hardened.

Sprinkle sponge cake with rum or liqueur. Pick over raspberries or strawberries, or peel and slice peaches, removing pits. Toss with sugar to taste, cover and let stand 15–30 minutes. Spread sides of cake with some whipped cream. Remove chocolate squares from wax paper with a small metal spatula and press them around the sides of the cake, overlapping slightly – top edges of the squares should come a little above the top of the cake.

Shortly before serving, spoon the fruit on top of cake and cover with remaining whipped cream, leaving a border of fruit.

HOW TO COOK SAUSAGES

There are hundreds of kinds of sausages. In Europe every country has its specialty, whether it is Italian salami or pepperoni, Spanish chorizo, French boudin and andouillettes, or the English fresh sausages known colloquially as bangers, because of their way of bursting in the pan when cooked too fast.

Germany, however, is the undisputed sausage center of the world. Knackwurst, Blutwurst, Bratwurst, Weisswurst (you will have guessed that 'wurst' means 'sausage') – the list of popular German sausages is long and includes dozens of lesser known varieties.

Basically a sausage is a mixture of ground, seasoned meat stuffed into a casing that gives it its long characteristic shape. Almost any kind of meat – veal, beef, pork, lamb or game – is used, although pork is the most common ingredient. Sausages make much from little, for their manufacture has long been recognized as an invaluable way of using up scraps of meat and parts of the animal – stomach lining, head and innards – that otherwise would be regarded as inedible. Traditionally the casings are made of animal intestines.

Sausages are typed not only by the meat used but by the predominant seasoning, which may range from mild to hot to almost sour. Combinations of seasonings vary from maker to maker, and many recipes are a jealously guarded secret.

Fresh sausages with relatively little seasoning, like country sausages, do not keep well and must be used within a few days. The more spice, salt and preservatives like saltpeter that they contain, the longer they can be kept. Many sausages are smoked, dried or completely cooked to improve their keeping qualities and smoking also adds an aromatic bouquet. Popular examples of partially or completely cooked sausages are liverwurst and bologna. Dried sausages like salami, pepperoni and cervelat, whether smoked or not, can be kept without refrigeration in a cool, dry place.

Depending on their type, sausages can be served in any number of ways – sliced for sandwiches on a platter of cold cuts or used as a spread; broiled, fried, baked or poached to serve hot. It is essential to cook sausages thoroughly, particularly those based on pork.

Key to Hanging Sausage Display

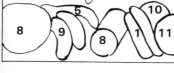

1 Smoked Linguiça

2 German salami

3 Genoa salami

4 Hungarian salami

5 Uncooked Spanish chorizo links

6 German Braunschweiger

7 Italian pepperoni

8 German Blutwurst

9 Landjäger links

10 Kosher salami

11 Italian hard salami

121

An appetizing plate of assorted sausages is garnished with wholewheat bread, scallion brushes, radish roses and olives. They are (in clockwise order from top center): Italian hard salami, a sliced link of Hungarian salami, German Blutwurst and Italian pepperoni

KINDS OF SAUSAGES

The following sausages are ready to eat unless otherwise stated.

Andouilles
Large sausage made of pig's chitterlings and stomach filled into the intestine. Often simmered in water or white wine and sliced to serve cold or may be fried or broiled to serve hot with mashed potatoes.

Andouillettes
Small andouilles.

Blutwurst (blood sausage)
Pig's blood studded with pork, tongue and other meat in large casings. Blutwurst is sold completely cooked and smoked or it may be fresh, when it must be thoroughly cooked before eating.

Bockwurst
Finely ground veal, sometimes with pork, delicately flavored with chives and parsley, and enriched with eggs and cream; packed in small casings and parboiled. Before eating poach Bockwurst for 10 minutes, then brush with butter and broil.

Berliner Bockwurst
This is a smoked sausage similar to a frankfurter.

Bologna
Finely ground cured pork and beef with aromatic seasonings, packed in large casings.

Boudin Blanc
Delicate sausage of finely ground pork or chicken, pork fat, bread, cream, eggs and sometimes goose liver or truffles. Generally broiled or fried in butter to serve hot.

Boudin Noir
Blood sausage of pork, pig's blood, suet, eggs, cream and onions. Cook like boudin blanc.

Bratwurst
Means pork sausage in German, though it may have veal added. Seasoned with sage and lemon juice; texture is coarse and it is usually broiled or fried for serving.

Braunschweiger
Braunschweig (Brunswick) is a town famous for its sausages, particularly Leberwurst (liver sausage) and Knackwurst. Braunschweiger Mettwurst is mildly smoked. Made of finely ground pork, it is soft enough to spread on crackers.

Cervelat
General term for mild dried sausages that need no cooking.

> **Farmer**: equal parts of coarsely chopped pork and beef with delicate seasoning and lightly smoked. Texture is rather soft.

> **Göteborg** (Swedish sausage): coarsely chopped pork and beef, salty and heavily smoked.

> **Göttinger**: dry and quite spicy.

> **Landjäger**: of Swiss origin, it is heavily smoked and dried until wrinkled and almost black.

> **Thüringer**: a mixture of pork and beef, flavored with coriander and mustard seed, often called summer sausage.

Chorizo
A Spanish sausage of coarsely chopped pork, colored and flavored with pimiento, red pepper and garlic, usually smoked. Often simmered in water or added to soup; also an important ingredient in paella.

Fleischwurst
Finely ground beef, pork and veal, lightly seasoned and smoked in large casings. Usually steamed to serve hot or cold or can be sliced and fried; some contain chicken. Must be cooked before serving.

Frankfurters (wieners)
America's most popular sausage; spiced and smoked and usually made of more pork than beef.

Kielbasa (Polish sausage)
Coarsely chopped pork mixed with beef and veal that is highly seasoned and lightly smoked. Broil or fry it to serve with mashed potatoes or sauerkraut or cook with sauerkraut.

Knackwurst
Short, fat sausages similar to frankfurters but seasoned with garlic.

Kolbascy
German version of kielbasa; contains more garlic and is often dried until it resembles salami. Usually poached or baked for serving.

Liver sausage (Leberwurst)
Soft, fully cooked mixture, usually of pork liver mixed with pork or veal. Possible seasonings include garlic, herbs, onions, anchovies, pistachios and almost any kind of spice.

Lyon Sausage
Finely ground pork with small cubes of pork fat; seasoned with spices and garlic; packed in large casings and dried. A specialty of Lyon, France.

Mortadella
Similar to Lyon sausage with large cubes of pork fat; flavored with anise, garlic and coriander.

Fresh Pork Sausage
Can be finely or coarsely ground and seasoning varies from mild to spicy; English pork sausages contain a relatively high proportion of bread which lightens their texture. They are usually broiled or fried. Pork sausage meat is also available loose without casings.

Salami
General term for highly seasoned dry sausage, sometimes smoked, with a slightly acid flavor. As the name suggests, most are of Italian origin.

> **Apennino**: coarsely chopped pork and beef is flavored with mustard as well as garlic, salt, pepper and sugar.

Arles: French salami similar to Milano but made of coarsely chopped meat.

Calabrese: pork salami seasoned with chilies.

Genoa, Italian, Milano: coarsely chopped cured pork with some finely chopped beef. Often made with wine or grape juice, flavored with garlic, and filled in large casings.

German: less highly flavored and more heavily smoked than Italian.

Hungarian: this is more heavily smoked than Italian.

Pepperoni: dried Italian sausages of coarsely ground pork and beef, flavored and colored with ground red pepper. Seasoning can vary from sweet to highly spiced.

Strasbourg Sausage
Very much like frankfurters and made with beef, pork and veal.

Summer Sausage
Usually refers to mildly seasoned cervelat but correctly includes all dry sausages — before refrigeration, most sausages were dried in summer so they kept better.

Weisswurst
Large Bockwurst, flavored with parsley, mace, sage and thyme.

MAKING SAUSAGES

Several types of sausages are easy to make at home and it is worth experimenting with recipes to achieve just the right balance of seasoning for your taste. All the equipment needed is a grinder with coarse and fine blades and a conical tube for stuffing. Some grinders have an attachment so the sausage mixture can be ground and filled into the casings at the same time.

Casings can be found in specialty meat markets and saltpeter, used as a preservative in some sausages, is available in drugstores.

To Prepare and Fill Sausage Casings

Most casings sold commercially have been cleaned and only need to be soaked in cold water for 2–4 hours before using. If they are not already cleaned, empty them, turn them inside out and wash well. Soak them for 6–8 hours in cold water with 1 tablespoon lye to 1 gallon water. Drain them, scrape away fat, wash well and turn right side out. Scrape outside and wash well also. Artificial casings need no preparation.

To fill the casings, insert the stuffer in one end and wrinkle the casings over it, like a stocking, until the other end is reached; knot the end or tie with string. Fill casings, letting casing slip off the stuffer gradually; twist or tie sausages with string in even lengths. Do not fill casings too full or they will burst during cooking.

Pork Sausages

4 lb pork shoulder, neck or
   trimmings
2 tablespoons salt
1 tablespoon coarsely ground
   black pepper
1½ tablespoons sage
1 teaspoon nutmeg
1 teaspoon sugar
small hog casings

Makes about 40 links.

The same mixture can be seasoned much more highly with ground mustard, cayenne, allspice and coriander. Often pork sausage meat is shaped into patties instead of being filled into casings.

Method
Work the pork through the coarse blade of the grinder — there should be about 3 parts meat to 1 part fat. Spread meat in a roasting pan and sprinkle with seasonings and sugar. Work the meat again through the grinder and fill it into casings. Tie or twist into 3–4 inch lengths and store in the refrigerator for up to 4 days.

To serve: broil or fry in a little oil until browned.

Work cubes of pork through a meat grinder, then season the ground mixture. Fix sausage-making attachment to the grinder and pull casings onto the attachment

Tie string at the end of the casing, grind meat again so the mixture fills the casing to make links. Tie or twist links to desired size

Boudin Blanc

2 cups cooked chicken meat or
  1 lb boneless uncooked
  chicken breasts
$1\frac{1}{2}$ lb lean pork
$1\frac{1}{2}$ lb pork fat
$1\frac{1}{2}$ tablespoons salt
2 teaspoons ground white
  pepper
2 teaspoons ground allspice
2 onions, finely chopped
6 eggs
1 cup fresh white breadcrumbs,
  soaked in 1 cup scalded
  cream
$\frac{1}{4}$ cup butter, melted (to serve)

For cooking
1 quart water
2 cups milk

Large sheep casings

Makes about 12 sausages.

Method
Work the chicken, pork and pork fat twice through the fine blade of the grinder. Spread the meat in a roasting pan, sprinkle over the salt, pepper, allspice and onions and work again through the grinder. Add the eggs, soaked breadcrumbs and cream and beat in an electric mixer if possible, for 5 minutes until the mixture comes away from the sides of the bowl. Fill into the casings and tie or twist in 6-inch lengths.

In a large pan bring the water and milk to a boil. Lower the sausages, preferably in a wire basket, and simmer very gently for 20 minutes. As the sausages rise to the surface, prick them with a needle to let out the air. Drain the sausages well and let cool. Store in refrigerator for up to 2 days.

To serve: brush with melted butter and broil; or sauté in melted butter. Serve with mashed potatoes.

Bockwurst

5 lb veal shoulder or trimmings
$\frac{1}{4}$ cup chopped chives
1 tablespoon salt
2 teaspoons sage
2 teaspoons ground white
  pepper
$1\frac{1}{2}$ teaspoons sugar
1 teaspoon ground mace
$\frac{1}{2}$ teaspoon ground cloves
few drops of lemon extract
3 eggs
1 cup cream

Small hog casings

Makes about 16 Bockwurst.

Method
Work the veal twice through the fine blade of the grinder and spread it out in a roasting pan. Sprinkle over the chives, salt, sage, pepper, sugar, mace, cloves and lemon extract. Add the eggs and cream and beat for 5 minutes, preferably in an electric mixer, until the mixture comes away from the sides of the bowl. Fill the mixture into the casings and tie or twist into 5–6 inch lengths.

Bring a kettle of heavily salted water to a boil. Lower in the sausages, preferably in a wire basket, and simmer very gently for 2–3 minutes. Let cool in the water, then drain. Store the Bockwurst in the refrigerator for up to 2 days.

To serve: simmer the Bockwurst in water for 10–15 minutes, drain and serve with bread and butter with sweet mustard as a seasoning.

Weisswurst

Follow the recipe for Bockwurst but fill into large sheep casings to make thinner sausages 3–4 inches long.

Knackwurst

1 lb lean beef
$2\frac{1}{2}$ tablespoons salt
scant teaspoon saltpeter
$1\frac{1}{2}$ lb lean pork
$\frac{1}{2}$ lb pork fat
2 large cloves garlic, crushed
1 tablespoon cumin seeds,
  crushed but not ground
2 teaspoons dried crushed red
  pepper
1 teaspoon black pepper,
  freshly ground
1 cup water
$\frac{1}{4}$ cup butter, melted (to serve)

Large sheep casings

Makes about 12 sausages.

Method
Work the beef through the fine blade of the grinder, spread it on a plate and sprinkle over the salt and saltpeter. Work the pork and pork fat through the coarse blade of the grinder and combine with the beef. Spread out the mixture, sprinkle over the garlic, cumin seeds, and red and black pepper. Beat well for 5 minutes, if possible in an electric mixer, until the mixture leaves the sides of the bowl; beat in the 1 cup water. Fill the casings and twist or tie in 4–5 inch lengths. Hang them in an airy room (about 60°F) and dry them for 2 to 5 days, depending on the humidity. Then smoke them for 2 to 5 hours until brown or dark mahogany, to your taste. Do not let the temperature rise above 100°F. Store for up to a month in the refrigerator.

Simmer in boiling water to cover for 12–15 minutes and drain; or split lengthwise, brush with butter and broil or sauté in butter. Serve with split pea or lentil purée (see page 109).

SAUSAGE DISHES

Sausage Soup

$\frac{3}{4}$ lb mild or hot Italian sausage
1 tablespoon oil
1 onion, chopped
2 tomatoes, peeled, seeded
  and chopped
1 clove garlic, crushed
$\frac{1}{2}$ teaspoon thyme
bay leaf
salt and pepper
6 cups water
small loaf French bread, sliced
  (for croûtes)
$\frac{1}{2}$ cup grated Parmesan cheese
  (for serving)

Method
In a kettle heat the oil and fry the sausages for 10–12 minutes or until thoroughly cooked and browned on all sides. Take them out, add the onion to the pan and cook until soft. Add the tomatoes, garlic, thyme, bay leaf and seasoning and cook, stirring, until the mixture is very soft and pulpy. Add the water, bring to a boil and boil 8–10 minutes.

To make croûtes: bake the bread in a moderate oven (350°F) until crisp and golden brown and place in a soup tureen or in individual bowls.

Cut the sausages in $\frac{1}{2}$ inch slices, add to the soup, bring just back to a boil and taste for seasoning. Spoon over the croûtes and serve grated cheese separately.

Sausages in Red Wine

1½ lb fresh pork sausages
1 tablespoon oil
¼ cup dry white breadcrumbs
1½ cups red wine
½ teaspoon thyme
1 bay leaf

Method

In a skillet heat the oil and fry the sausages gently for 4–5 minutes until browned on all sides, pricking them so they do not burst. Pour off all but 3 tablespoons fat, add the breadcrumbs and cook, stirring, until browned. Add the wine and herbs and simmer until the wine is reduced by half and forms a sauce. Discard the bay leaf and transfer sausages and sauce to a serving dish. Serve with lentil (see page 109) or chestnut purée.

Chestnut Purée

2 lb chestnuts, peeled
1 stalk of celery
bouquet garni
2 cups stock
¼ cup butter
¼ teaspoon allspice
salt and pepper

Method

In a saucepan cook chestnuts with celery, bouquet garni and stock until boiling; cover and simmer 45 minutes or until the chestnuts are very tender but not mushy. Drain them, discard the celery and bouquet garni and work chestnuts through a sieve or food mill, or purée in a blender with a little cooking liquid.

Return purée to pan and beat in butter over heat. Season with allspice and salt and pepper to taste. Purée should be light and not sticky.

Blutwurst with Apples

1–1½ lb Blutwurst, boudin noir or other uncooked blood sausages
1 tablespoon oil
4–5 tart apples, peeled, cored and sliced
2 teaspoons sugar
salt and pepper

Method

Cut the sausages in 1 inch slices or leave whole, according to size. In a shallow flameproof casserole heat the oil and fry the sausages for 8–10 minutes until thoroughly cooked and browned on all sides. Remove them and keep warm. Add the sliced apples to the pan with the sugar and seasoning and stir so they are well coated with fat. Cook over medium heat, stirring occasionally, for 4–5 minutes or until the apples are tender and lightly browned. Set the sausages on top and serve.

Italian Sausage with Chicory

1½ lb mild or hot Italian sausages
1 head chicory, washed and chopped
salt
black pepper, freshly ground

Method

Put the sausages in a skillet with 1–2 tablespoons water and cook gently for 10–12 minutes until thoroughly cooked and brown on all sides, pricking them so they do not burst. Take them out and keep warm. Pour off all but 2 tablespoons fat and add the chicory with 2 tablespoons water and seasoning (use very little pepper if the sausages are hot). Cover and cook 15–20 minutes until tender, stirring occasionally. Pile the chicory in a serving dish, cut the sausages in 2–3 inch diagonal slices and pile on top.

Choucroute Alsacienne (Sauerkraut with Pork and Sausages)

3 lb fresh or canned sauerkraut
1 lb Kielbasa or other garlic sausages
4 Knackwurst or frankfurter sausages
4 Swiss Schublig sausages
1 lb piece lean bacon
¼ cup butter
2 onions, chopped
12 juniper berries, crushed
2 cloves garlic, crushed
black pepper, freshly ground
1 cup white wine
1–2 cups stock
6–8 thinly cut smoked pork chops
1 lb Canadian bacon, cut in thick slices
¼ cup kirsch

Serves 10–12 people.

Method

Blanch the lean bacon by putting it in cold water, bringing to a boil and simmering 2 minutes. Drain and cut it in slices, discarding any rind. Drain fresh sauerkraut, soak in cold water for 15 minutes, then drain and press dry with your hands; if using canned sauerkraut, drain, rinse and press it dry. Pull the sauerkraut apart with your fingers so it does not form lumps.

In a large flameproof casserole, melt the butter and fry the onion until soft but not browned. Add the sauerkraut, juniper berries, garlic and plenty of pepper and mix well.

Pour in wine and half the stock, lay slices of bacon on top, cover and bake in a moderately low oven (325°F) for 2 hours. Add the smoked pork chops and garlic sausages, burying them well in the sauerkraut, and pour in more stock if necessary – the sauerkraut should be moist but not covered with liquid. Cover and continue cooking 30 minutes. Add the sliced Canadian bacon and Knackwurst or frankfurter sausages and Swiss Schublig sausages and continue cooking 30 minutes or until all the meats are cooked.

Cut the garlic sausage in 1 inch diagonal slices and replace it in the pan. Pour over the kirsch and taste the sauerkraut for seasoning – if the sauerkraut was mildly pickled, it may need salt. Serve the sauerkraut in the casserole with the meats or pile it in the center of a platter and arrange the meats around it. Serve boiled potatoes separately.

The heart-warming qualities of choucroute Alsacienne are renowned

Kielbasa with Cabbage

1½ lb Kielbasa sausages, cut in
  ½ inch diagonal slices
1 head Savoy or green cabbage,
  shredded
3 slices of bacon, diced
1 onion, sliced
1 teaspoon caraway seeds
1 teaspoon sugar
juice of ½ lemon
salt and pepper
2 tablespoons water
1 potato

Method

In a flameproof casserole fry the bacon until browned, drain and reserve it. Add the sliced sausages and fry until browned on all sides. Add the onion and cook until soft. Add the shredded cabbage, caraway seeds, sugar, lemon juice and seasoning, and mix well.

Add water, cover the pan and simmer gently 5–8 minutes. Peel and grate the potato and stir into the cabbage – the potato disintegrates and thickens the mixture slightly. Cover and continue cooking 15 minutes or until the cabbage is tender, stirring occasionally. Serve in the casserole, with boiled potatoes separately.

Bratwurst with Chestnuts

1½ lb Bratwurst
1½ lb chestnuts, peeled
2 tablespoons oil
1 onion, finely sliced
1½ cups stock
¼ cup water

Method

In a flameproof casserole heat 1 tablespoon oil and fry the onion until soft but not browned. Add the chestnuts and stock, cover and simmer 20–25 minutes until the chestnuts are almost tender. The stock should be almost absorbed but if not, remove the lid during the last few minutes' cooking.

In a skillet heat the remaining oil and gently fry the Bratwurst for 8–10 minutes until browned on all sides. Add the water and shake the pan to dissolve the juices in the bottom. Add the chestnuts and continue cooking, stirring occasionally, for 5 minutes or until the pan juices are absorbed by the chestnuts. Serve with braised red cabbage.

Sausage Pie

1 lb sausage meat
2 tablespoons oil
2 onions, chopped
4–5 tomatoes, peeled, seeded
  and chopped or 3 cups
  canned tomatoes, crushed
1 green pepper, cored, seeded
  and chopped
1 teaspoon paprika
½ teaspoon chili powder
salt
rich pie pastry, made with 1 cup
  flour, pinch of salt, ⅓ cup
  butter, 1 egg yolk, 1–2
  tablespoons water
1 egg, beaten to mix with
  ½ teaspoon salt (for glaze)

Deep 9 inch pie pan

Method

Make the pie pastry dough and chill 30 minutes. Set the oven at hot (400°F).

Roll the sausage meat into walnut-sized balls and fry them in a skillet in 1 tablespoon oil until browned on all sides. Arrange them in the pie pan. Fry the onions in the remaining oil until lightly browned, add the tomatoes, green pepper, paprika, chili powder, and a little salt and simmer, stirring occasionally, for 5–8 minutes until the mixture is pulpy. Spoon it over the sausage balls and let cool.

Roll out the pastry and cover the pie; flute the edges of the pastry and pierce a hole in the center for steam to escape. Brush with egg glaze and bake in the heated oven for 15 minutes or until beginning to brown; turn oven down to moderate (350°F) and continue baking 15–20 minutes or until the pastry is well browned and the pie is very hot.

Sausage Kebabs

1½ lb sausage meat
2 teaspoons crushed bay leaf
2 finely chopped shallots or
  scallions
¼ cup melted butter (for
  brushing)

8 kebab skewers

Method

Mix the sausage meat thoroughly with the bay leaf and shallots or scallions. Shape the mixture into walnut-sized balls and spear them on kebab skewers. Brush them with melted butter and broil, preferably over charcoal, for 8–10 minutes or until browned and thoroughly cooked, turning the kebabs and brushing with butter during broiling. Serve with rice pilaf and baked apples with apricot (see page 62).

Hot Garlic Sausage with Potato Salad

1–1½ lb Lyon, Kielbasa or other
  garlic sausages

For potato salad
4–5 medium potatoes
6 tablespoons olive oil
2–3 tablespoons white wine
  vinegar
salt and pepper
1 tablespoon chopped chives
  or 2 shallots, chopped

Method

Cook the sausages in simmering water for 15–20 minutes.

To make the potato salad: cook the potatoes in their skins in boiling salted water for 15–20 minutes or until just tender. Peel and slice them while still hot and put them in a bowl. Sprinkle over the oil, vinegar, seasoning and chives or shallots and mix carefully.

Drain the sausages, cut in ½-inch diagonal slices and serve with the warm potato salad.

Liver Sausage Salad

1 lb liver sausage, sliced
4 tomatoes, peeled and sliced
1 head chicory, washed and torn into leaves

For dressing
3 tablespoons wine vinegar
½ teaspoon Dijon-style mustard
salt
black pepper, freshly ground
3 tablespoons oil
½ cup heavy cream

To finish
1 tablespoon chopped capers
1 hard-cooked egg, finely chopped
1 tablespoon chopped parsley

Method
To make the dressing: whisk the vinegar with the mustard and seasoning, and gradually beat in the oil until the mixture emulsifies and thickens slightly. Gradually beat in the cream.

Arrange the sausage and tomato slices, overlapping, around the edge of a deep platter and spoon over a little of the dressing. Toss the chicory with the remaining dressing and pile in the center. Sprinkle the capers on the tomatoes and sausage and the egg and parsley on the chicory.

Chorizo Salad

½ lb chorizo sausages, thinly sliced
½ lb green beans, cooked and cut in 2-inch lengths
1 cup cooked corn kernels or 1 can (8 oz) corn kernels, drained
3 cooked potatoes, diced
2 tomatoes, peeled, seeded and cut in strips
small head Boston or romaine lettuce, divided in leaves and washed
paprika (for sprinkling)

For dressing
3 tablespoons wine vinegar
¼ teaspoon cayenne
1 clove garlic, crushed
salt
black pepper, freshly ground
⅓ cup olive oil

Method
To make the dressing: whisk the vinegar with the cayenne, garlic and salt and pepper. Gradually whisk in the oil so the mixture thickens slightly and emulsifies.

In a bowl mix the chorizo sausages, green beans, corn, potatoes and tomatoes. Add the dressing, mix well and taste for seasoning. Cover and chill at least 2 hours so the flavors mellow.

To serve: arrange the lettuce leaves around a salad bowl, pile the sausage mixture in the center and sprinkle with paprika.

Cervelat Salad

1 lb cervelat or summer sausage, thinly sliced
1 Bermuda or other mild onion, thinly sliced
2 hard-cooked eggs, cut in wedges
2 tomatoes, peeled and cut in 8 wedges
3 dill pickles, cut in quarters lengthwise
1 tablespoon chopped parsley (for garnish)

For dressing
2 teaspoons prepared mustard
2 cloves of garlic, crushed
2 tablespoons mayonnaise
salt and pepper
½ cup cider vinegar
½ cup oil

Method
To make the dressing: stir the mustard and garlic into the mayonnaise with the seasoning. Stir in the vinegar, then gradually whisk in the oil so the dressing emulsifies and thickens slightly. Taste for seasoning.

Arrange the sausage and onion slices, overlapping, in a dish, spoon over the dressing, cover and let marinate from 2–8 hours.

A short time before serving, arrange the eggs, tomatoes and dill pickles around the dish. Sprinkle with chopped parsley.

Italian Sausage Salad

1½ lb mild or hot Italian sausage
1 large cauliflower, divided into sprigs
1 large mild or Bermuda onion, very thinly sliced
1 teaspoon basil
1 tablespoon chopped parsley

For dressing
¼ cup wine vinegar
1 clove of garlic, crushed
1 tablespoon tomato paste
½ cup olive oil
salt
black pepper, freshly ground

Method
Put the sausages in a skillet with 1–2 tablespoons water and cook gently for 10–12 minutes or until thoroughly cooked and brown on all sides, pricking them so they do not burst. Let them cool, then cut in 1-inch diagonal slices.

Cook the cauliflower in boiling salted water for 8–10 minutes or until just tender, drain and let cool.

To make the dressing: gradually whisk the vinegar into the garlic and tomato paste, then whisk in the olive oil with the seasoning, a little at a time so the dressing emulsifies and thickens slightly.

Combine the sausages, onion slices and cauliflower in a bowl and toss well with dressing. Sprinkle with basil and parsley and chill ½–1 hour before serving.

HIGH ALTITUDE COOKING

Cooking at high altitudes (at elevations above 3,000 feet) is the same as anywhere else, except for two essential adjustments. The time needed for boiling foods must be increased and the proportions of ingredients used in leavened foods must be modified.

The boiling point of water, which at sea level is 212°F, declines to 203°F at an altitude of 5,000 feet. Consequently, anything cooked in liquid — whether boiled, braised, simmered or steamed — requires a longer cooking time since the heat is lower than it would be at sea level.

The effect of high altitudes on baking is more complicated. Not only do cooking times change, but also adjustments are made to ingredient proportions and oven temperatures. Doughs and batters tend to rise more rapidly so it is often necessary to decrease the amount of leavening agent and, because of faster evaporation, use more liquid and less sugar and increase the oven temperature by 10°F–15°F. At highest altitudes, more eggs are often required, but they should not be over beaten as this can result in a dry cake. In cake baking the use of self-rising flour is not recommended.

High altitude has its strongest effect on the rising time of bread. When baking bread at high altitudes, the rising period is shortened. However, the nut-like flavor of good home baked bread is developed from the length of the rising period, so it is advisable to allow your bread two risings so the flavor can develop.

Occasionally there are problems at altitudes above 5,000 feet when using cornstarch as a thickening agent. Because of the lower boiling point of liquids it is, therefore, necessary to use direct heat rather than a double boiler when making puddings, creams and sauces.

For deep fat frying, it is necessary to lower the temperature of the fat by 10°F–15°F to compensate for the lower boiling point of the liquids in the food being fried.

The charts shown at right will help you in your cooking at high altitudes, but for best results, it is wise to contact your local Home Extension Service, the Home Economics Department of your State College or your local utility company for specialized information for your own area.

Cake Recipe Adjustment Guide for High Altitudes

Adjustment	3,000 feet	5,000 feet	7,000 feet
Reduce baking powder **For each teaspoon, decrease**	$\frac{1}{8}$ teaspoon	$\frac{1}{8}-\frac{1}{4}$ teaspoon	$\frac{1}{4}$ teaspoon
Reduce sugar **For each cup, decrease**	0–1 tablespoon	0–2 tablespoons	1–3 tablespoons
Increase liquid **For each cup add**	1–2 tablespoons	2–4 tablespoons	3–4 tablespoons

Approximate Boiling Temperatures of Water at Various Altitudes

Boiling point of water	Altitude				
	Sea Level	2,000 feet	5,000 feet	7,500 feet	10,000 feet
Degrees F	212	208	203	198	194
Degrees C	100	98	95	92	90

MEASURING & MEASUREMENTS

The recipe quantities in the Course are measured in standard level teaspoons, tablespoons and cups and their equivalents are shown below. Any liquid pints and quarts also refer to U.S. standard measures.

When measuring dry ingredients, fill the cup or spoon to overflowing without packing down and level the top with a knife. All the dry ingredients, including flour, should be measured before sifting, although sifting may be called for later in the instructions.

Butter and margarine usually come in measured sticks (1 stick equals $\frac{1}{2}$ cup) and other bulk fats can be measured by displacement. For $\frac{1}{3}$ cup fat, fill the measuring cup $\frac{2}{3}$ full of water. Add fat until the water reaches the 1 cup mark. Drain the cup of water and the fat remaining equals $\frac{1}{3}$ cup.

For liquids, fill the measure to the brim, or to the calibration line.

Often quantities of seasonings cannot be stated exactly, for ingredients vary in the amount they require. The instructions 'add to taste' are literal, for it is impossible to achieve just the right balance of flavors in many dishes without tasting them.

Liquid measure	Volume equivalent
3 teaspoons	1 tablespoon
2 tablespoons	1 fluid oz
4 tablespoons	$\frac{1}{4}$ cup
16 tablespoons	1 cup or 8 fluid oz
2 cups	1 pint
2 pints	1 quart
4 quarts	1 gallon

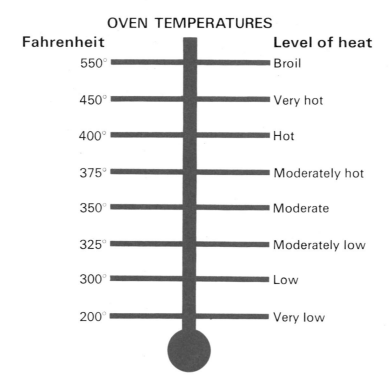

OVEN TEMPERATURES

Fahrenheit	Level of heat
550°	Broil
450°	Very hot
400°	Hot
375°	Moderately hot
350°	Moderate
325°	Moderately low
300°	Low
200°	Very low

OVEN TEMPERATURES AND SHELF POSITIONS

Throughout the Cooking Course, oven temperatures are stated in degrees Fahrenheit and in generally agreed levels of heat such as 'high' and 'moderate'. The equivalents are shown on the table above.

However, exact temperature varies in different parts of an oven and the thermostat reading refers to the heat in the middle. As the oven temperature at top and bottom can vary as much as 25°F from this setting, the positioning of shelves is very important. In general, heat rises, so the hottest part of the oven is at the top, but consult the manufacturer's handbook about your individual model.

Pans and dishes of food should be placed parallel with burners or elements to avoid scorched edges.

When baking cakes, there must be room for the heat to circulate in the oven around baking sheets and cake pans; otherwise the underside of the cakes will burn. If baking more than one cake in an oven that has back burners or elements, arrange the cakes side by side. If the oven has side burners, arrange cakes back and front.

Oven thermostats are often inaccurate and are unreliable at extremely high or low temperatures. If you do a great deal of baking or question the accuracy of your oven, use a separate oven thermometer as a check on the thermostat.

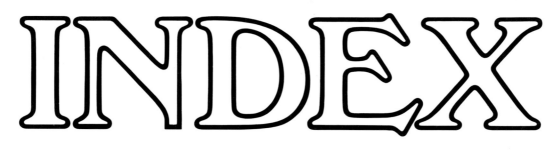

(Volume 12)

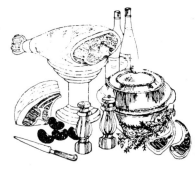

V

Y

W

Acknowledgments
Photographs by Fred J. Maroon on pages 8, 11, 12, 13, 14, 16, 18, 19, 21, 26, 27, 29, 68, 82, 86, 89 and 97. Photographs by Ross Chapple on pages 120, 122, 125, 126 and 129; styling by Fay Abell. Photographs on pages 41 and 98 by PAF/C. Délu. Other photographs by Michael Leale, John Ledger and Roger Phillips.